Another Mother
Co-parenting with the Foster Care System

Another Mother

CO-PARENTING WITH THE FOSTER CARE SYSTEM

Sarah Gerstenzang

Vanderbilt University Press
Nashville

10 09 08 07   1 2 3 4 5

Printed on acid-free paper.
Manufactured in the United States of America
Designed by Gary Gore

Library of Congress Cataloging-in-Publication Data

Gerstenzang, Sarah.
Another mother : co-parenting with the foster care system /
Sarah Gerstenzang.—1st ed.
p. cm.
Includes bibliographical references and index.
ISBN-13: 978-0-8265-1548-3 (cloth : alk. paper)
ISBN-13: 978-0-8265-1549-0 (pbk. : alk. paper)
1. Foster parents—United States—Biography.
2. Foster mothers—United States—Biography.
3. Foster children—United States.
4. Foster home care—United States.
5. Adopted children—United States. I. Title.
HQ759.7.G47 2007
362.73'3—dc22
2006029489

To Emma, Lily, and Sam

Contents

Acknowledgments

This book is about families. I could not have written it without help from mine. My husband, Michael, was there for me in every way—encouraging me, listening and responding to ideas, reading drafts, and taking over the parenting on many Saturdays so that I could work on this project. My sister, Elisabeth Sheffield, taught me about writing and about how to put a book together. And my brother-in-law, John Allen, encouraged me to begin this project and provided me with editing and advice along the way. I am grateful too to my mother, Patricia Ackerman, who read the manuscript and provided encouragement and to my sister, Stephanie Sheffield, and my brother-in-law, Jeffrey DeShell, who provided love and support.

There are a number of others I am indebted to who read the manuscript and provided me with generous feedback and support: Madelyn Freundlich, Jennine Meyer, Leslee Morris, Emily Fenichel, Peggy Porter Tierney, Evelyn Rothbard, Regina Diehl, Deborah Dentler, and Alexandra Lowe. And Emily Berger, who provided much encouragement over many cups of coffee.

Finally, I thank my editor at Vanderbilt University Press, Michael Ames, for his enthusiastic support.

Foreword

The contours of the child-welfare system in this country appear to be well defined by law and policy. Yet we have gleaned from the experiences of those directly affected by that system that it is fraught with tensions, conflicting values, and uncertainties that often undermine the achievement of the very goals the system was designed to accomplish. The ways in which the realities of foster care affect children, their parents, and their caregivers have not always been clear, however, because we have not often heard the voices of those who receive and provide foster care services. We have not had many opportunities to hear directly from parents whose children have been removed from them and placed in foster care, children who find themselves in a system that often places them with families they do not know, foster parents who are asked to provide security, nurturance, and love while at the same time not to become "overly attached" to the children entrusted to them, and foster parents who go on to adopt the children with whom they have·fallen in love.

Because these voices largely have been absent, we have been able to cling to a belief that law, policy, and practice govern foster care and the adoption of children from foster care relatively smoothly. We can be heartened by statistics that indicate that fewer children are entering foster care, that children are remaining in care for shorter periods of time, and that more children are being adopted. Certainly, these indicators provide hopeful "big picture" signs that children's and families' experiences with the foster care system are increasingly positive, and they suggest that the system is working fairly well. What these statistics do not and cannot provide, however, is an understanding of the day-to-day experiences of those whose lives are interwoven with the foster care system, who must navigate its complexities and its challenges, and for whom joy and satisfaction are in delicate balance with heartbreak and frustration.

The enactment of the federal Adoption and Safe Families Act of 1997 (ASFA) marked a sea change in foster care practice. Under the new law, states were required to move more quickly to achieve permanence for children in foster care, working toward their safe reunification with their parents or, when that goal could not be achieved relatively quickly, freeing them for adoption and placing them with adoptive families. To achieve permanency quickly, foster care systems across the country implemented many changes, including an examination of the role of foster parents and a new planning approach, concurrent planning, which simultaneously considered two potential permanency outcomes for children: reunification and adoption. To implement this approach, foster parents were asked to serve dual roles: to care for children and support their safe return to their parents when possible and, at the same time, to stand ready to adopt children if reunification could not be accomplished within legally designated timelines. The theory was sound: This approach would promote children's well-being by placing them with families who could serve as both a foster family and a prospective adoptive family, eliminating repeated changes in children's lives.

The realities of this practice, however, multiplied the complexity of the role foster parents were already expected to play. They raised numerous systemic questions: How are foster parents to be recruited and supported to promote children's reunification with parents, becoming not too attached yet sufficiently attached to adopt the child if reunification does not occur? What is reasonable to expect of foster parents in their interactions with birth parents? What supports are provided to foster parents to navigate the many complex systems involved in their children's lives—not only the foster care system but also the legal system, the Medicaid system, and the Early Intervention and/or educational system? And if adoption becomes the plan for the child, how are foster parents supported in making the right decision for the child and for themselves?

Another Mother: Co-parenting with the Foster Care System offers a unique perspective on these and many other issues that characterize the foster care system in the wake of ASFA—the insight of a foster and adoptive mother who not only relates her own experiences as she and her family moved into the complex world of foster care and adoption but also shares her understanding, as a professional social worker, of the broader policy and practice environment in which her experiences played out. *Another Mother* pulls us not just into the life of one family but into the broader world of foster care and adoption practice and policy and into larger societal issues—racism, classism, and economic disparities—that provide the backdrop for the involvement of child-welfare systems across the country in the lives of children and families. *Another Mother* offers the often unheard voice of a foster and adoptive parent whose experiences bring to life the tensions, conflicting values, and uncertainties of the foster care system, as well as the triumphs and joys of a family whose life is now enriched by a beautiful new daughter.

—Madelyn Freundlich,
Child Welfare Consultant

Another Mother
Co-parenting with the Foster Care System

"Become a Foster Parent:
Help a Child"

IT WAS MIDNIGHT, February 28, 2000, a Monday on the verge of a Tuesday. I lay in bed, shivering from anxiety. Although I had wondered if I should stay dressed for the visitors I was expecting, I had decided to change into my pajamas to help myself relax. My two children—Peter, nine, and Martha, six and a half—were fast asleep upstairs in their bedrooms. My husband, Michael, was away on business in Chicago, just for the night. I kept wishing he was home with me.

The doorbell rang at 12:30 AM. I walked through the hall and down the stairs, my footsteps silenced by the carpeting under my bare feet. As if in a dream, I opened the front door to the cold night air. Our street, lined with brownstones and alive in the daytime with traffic and people walking children and dogs, was perfectly quiet, the only light thrown by streetlamps. Two strangers, an African American man and woman, stood on the doorstep. The man was cradling a tiny bundle wrapped in a soft white blanket. Seeing this couple so neatly and professionally dressed for work at my front door in the middle of the night added to my sense that I had entered another realm—where it is someone's job to take children from their own unsafe homes and place them with another family where they will be safe. Nothing about this situation was familiar to me.

My sense of the surreal was displaced by my desire to see inside that soft white bundle. I invited my visitors to the living room, where we all sat down on my overstuffed green velvet sofa and armchairs. Trying to appear generous, I offered to take their coats, but they said they wouldn't be staying. I wanted the bundle but the man did not offer it to me. Sensing his hesitation, I wondered if it was because I was white, because he felt sorry for the birth mother, or because he already felt attached to the baby himself. So I reached for the bundle, took my foster daughter into my arms, and felt the soft weight of her almost nine pounds. Inside the blanket, her head was covered with the hood of a matching white fleece snowsuit. I looked down at her face and she gazed straight back at me, her large brown eyes wide open. Experience told me that, at five weeks, she was too young to understand the precariousness of her situation. But searching for something, a clue to who she was, I thought I saw sadness in those eyes.

I signed some paperwork without reading it. I was given a copy of the "Administration for Children's Services Preplacement Services Fact Sheet Report" and the nurse triage form that confirmed the baby's name was Cecilia and that as of ten o'clock that night she was medically cleared with the exception of a diaper rash. The man and woman said a courteous goodbye, gave a little good luck pat to the bundle, and walked off into the night. As I shut the door, I caught sight of the large white van parked by the fire hydrant. My thoughts raced: Temporary parking because they don't intend to stay, this child is my responsibility now . . . Such a large van, how many children could they fit in that thing? . . . Looks like a commercial vehicle but it's anonymous—no large block letters on its side announcing "Administration for Children's Services: Rescuers of Abused and Neglected Children."

I carried the baby up to my bedroom, where I had hastily assembled a bassinet and some other necessities earlier that day. I laid Cecilia gently on my bed and, alone now, took my time examining her, feeling her downy-soft jet-black hair, getting to know her. I changed her from the Administration for Children's Services thin but new clothing into a white cotton T-shirt and a cozy blue sleeper that had belonged to a friend's daughter. Between outfits I paused, looking for clues, which I didn't find, that might help me understand why a child would be taken from her mother in the middle of the night. She had the diaper rash—nothing oozing and nasty, although the loss of pigment on her brown skin could have been a clue to some neglect in her first five weeks. But it was only a diaper rash. They don't remove children for that, do they?

The handoff had been so unofficial and mysterious that I was uncertain. When Martha and Peter were born, I saw them examined directly by the doctors, and that gave me confidence. As I examined Cecilia from head to toe, I noticed something on the upper fold of her tiny ear—my mind leapt—a cigarette burn? When I looked more closely, I saw that it was only a little indent, a natural mark that I would learn was formed in utero and completely harmless. (I later met an adult with the same indent on her ear, who said her grandmother told her it was the mark of an angel's kiss.) I reviewed the contents of the clear plastic bag the caseworkers had left with me—a can of formula, some ointment for the diaper rash, some clothing (several sizes too large) I assumed Cecilia was wearing when she was picked up, and a bottle with partly drunk formula and "I love my Mommy" written in pink on its side.

I kept expecting the baby to cry, but she didn't. She seemed completely alert and content. So I settled her into the bassinet, right next to the bed. I had rolled a towel up at the top so her head wouldn't hit the edge, and I covered her with a tiny down comforter and a green wool blanket that my mother had knit when Martha was born. I had no idea how much she would eat or when, but I decided to figure it out when she cried to tell me that she was hungry.

I called Michael at the hotel in Chicago. He asked me what she looked like and where she was at the moment. He sounded excited and eager to get home. It was difficult to describe to him how our entire lives had just changed with the ring of the doorbell. Seeing this baby, holding her, feeling her warmth and the softness of her skin, looking into her bright brown eyes and feeling her little breaths of air on my neck as I held her upright was so different from talking in the abstract about becoming foster parents, as we had on occasion for years and intensely for the last few months. I urged Michael to come home quickly but, just as I had savored the time alone in the hospital with Peter and Martha after their births, I clung to this time in the night with my foster daughter—just the two of us and no one else in the world. It was time not to react or plan or think but to be in the moment.

Cecilia hardly cried that first night but I didn't fall asleep until five o'clock. Martha, her face filled with magic and enthusiasm, woke me at 6:30, unable to contain her excitement at seeing the bassinet and the infant nestled inside. At seven, after waking Peter and holding the baby, she called "Mommy's mom" to share her joyful news.

I have wanted to have children for as long as I can remember—I believe I started thinking about this at about the same time I realized that my mother wasn't going to have any more (I was one of four) and that my desire to parent would be fulfilled only when I was old enough to have my own. Michael and I met at the end of high school, married at twenty-four, and had two children before we were thirty—young by today's standards. The pregnancies were horrific initially, as a result of excessive vomiting and nausea. During the second one, I lost so much weight that the doctor began to weigh me weekly and told me that unless I could manage to keep down "half a sandwich" I would have to be admitted to the hospital. I vowed to my husband, my sisters, and anyone else who would listen that I would never become pregnant again.

It is hard to say what sparked our interest in becoming foster parents. I had always been interested in adoption. I didn't necessarily want to be pregnant (although I loved giving birth)—it was simply the easiest path to having children. I knew that if I hadn't been able to bear children, I would have had no trouble with the concept of adoption. Michael felt the same way. However, we already had two terrific children. It was fascinating to see our genes mixed into two separate and entirely independent humans. And at some level, I wouldn't have minded seeing what the next child or the next twenty children looked like and were like. But there was over time a nagging interest in foster care, a topic that I generated that was of interest to Michael as well.

Our interest may have come in part from our own experience. Michael and I come from nontraditional families. Both of us had parents who divorced while we were young, and Michael was raised in part by a stepfather who never married his mother. My own mother remarried when I was eleven. When Michael was a year old and his mother was hospitalized during her pregnancy with his brother and separated from their father, he went to live with a friend of his mother and her two daughters for five months. Their ongoing bond was obvious almost twenty years later, when during a fall visit to Michael at his college, I noticed a Halloween card one of the daughters had sent him. It was slightly babyish to send to a college student but sweet at the same time. The inclusion of nonblood relatives in each of our childhoods gave us more fluid but eventually more stable home environments. While having stepfathers caused more complicated family dynamics for us, we both felt that we benefited from their care because of the extra emotional and financial support.

As with most women who divorce, our mothers experienced real poverty and we remembered the times, as children, when it was a struggle to make ends meet. However, because of stable family support and good educational opportunities, Michael and I now had a comfortable life together. And we felt grateful. We felt foster care was a way that we could give back to society—and we shared a conviction that high-quality, loving care would be beneficial to a child even if it was only for a short time.

My desire for a larger family also stemmed from other, selfish reasons. We loved our two biological children's early years and we thought we would enjoy another child's early years—especially as more seasoned parents. And I loved the dynamics of my own large family (the multilevel interaction, the differing personalities, the stimulation) while growing up. I wanted that for my own two children.

In looking through old correspondence between Michael and me when we were in college, I found a letter where I had written about an encounter with a child who was in foster care. One of the ways I earned money in college was babysitting. At the time, I was living with a family and babysitting for their five-year-old daughter, Claire, in exchange for living in their basement apartment. Among my responsibilities was taking Claire to her swimming lessons. One day while at the pool, I saw a boy who seemed to be about the same age as Claire. He must have looked a little lost because I asked him if he was with his parents. He replied in a bold voice: "I ain't got no parents. I'm a foster kid. I'm here with a worker." I wrote Michael, "I wanted to adopt him." Of course,

I didn't really, as I was just getting started in life myself. However, I did empathize strongly with his need for an everyday parent—I couldn't bear the idea that this boy was without parents.

Michael and I felt ready to provide some stability for a child who had none. We felt we understood what it took to be parents, having spent years parenting our two children. We knew how to be consistent, to be loving, and to gear activities to the age of a child to help him learn. And we enjoyed watching children develop, to see their personalities emerging and their competencies grow. We felt it was rewarding to be a part of that process.

When we were living in Brussels, we had our first experience with temporary care of a child in need. We were in Belgium on a two-and-a-half-year assignment for my husband's international law practice; Peter was then four and Martha was one and a half. I saw an ad one day in the *Bulletin*, an English-language weekly, about a group called SEMYA that was bringing Russian orphans to Belgium for the Christmas and summer holidays. The ad noted that the group needed more temporary families to house children. We signed up for the program, were interviewed during a home visit, and for two weeks in December, we housed, fed, and entertained Tatiana, who turned eight on the day she returned to Russia.

We felt the experience was a success—Tatiana seemed happy in our care and had medical, dental, and ophthalmology appointments during her visit. It was satisfying to introduce her to new experiences. Tatiana would hesitate to try new foods, then venture a small bite. Frequently a smile of pleasure followed—we lost count of how many clementine oranges Tatiana devoured. Once when I gave her a banana, she took a bite of the skin, then gamely tried again once I demonstrated that bananas need to be peeled first. We also enjoyed Tatiana's enthusiasm for activities she probably didn't get to do very much at home, like swimming.

At the end of two weeks, we were only getting to know Tatiana but it was hard to say goodbye, not sure whether we would ever see her again. A friend once asked whether two weeks with us was of any benefit to Tatiana. I couldn't say. One thing that made it easier to say goodbye was that she seemed like a happy well-adjusted child, and we reasoned that she must have someone who cares for her in Russia. For more than a year, I mailed her small packages with pictures and inexpensive items—mail in Russia at that time was very unreliable and there was always a risk that your package would be stolen—but we never heard from or about Tatiana again.

This brief experience helped shape our feelings about becoming foster parents. Language had been an obvious problem with Tatiana, as we did not speak any Russian and Tatiana spoke neither English nor French. Tatiana had been happier and better adjusted than we had expected a child from a Russian orphanage to be. We realized we would have more insight into the situations of children in need from our own country. With Tatiana, we learned that taking in a child who was older than our own was difficult, as we had no experience parenting a child of this age, nor did we have any toys or activities in place to entertain her. When I took Tatiana to our neighborhood pool and watched her splash and play, I was touched by her joy. She was passionate about swimming in a way that only a child who is deprived of ordinary activities might be. But I was also overwhelmed because it was difficult to entertain a four-year-old and a one-year-old by the side of the pool, as they got cold after fifteen or twenty minutes in the water. The experience with Tatiana taught us that two small children at one time were enough to manage.

We also underestimated the significance of birth order. Peter was used to being the oldest, and Tatiana was not used to having younger siblings. If Martha paid attention to Tatiana, Peter would be jealous because he was used to having Martha's undivided attention. I could see that Tatiana wanted my attention as well—eight had seemed old to me, but it is only old in comparison to a four-year-old, and she was still really a small child. The low point of the visit was a physical altercation between Tatiana and Peter in which he bit her and I had to mediate using hand signals. Michael and I decided to wait a few years before taking another child into our family.

Four years later, in January 1999, we were living in Brooklyn, New York. Peter was eight and Martha was six. I had gone to school part-time for the previous three years, and I was finishing up my master's in social work. We felt the time was right to look seriously into becoming foster parents. I was still home a lot because of the kids, and we thought if we waited much longer, we might feel too liberated from the bonds of family routine to take in a young child. We also took into consideration that I would have to spend some time getting a child settled and taking her or him to appointments, which would be difficult once I graduated and took a job.

We felt that it was now or never, but I was uncertain how to begin the process. I didn't know one other foster parent and I had never seen anything in my neighborhood about becoming one. I looked up "social services" in the yellow pages and called two agencies not too far away that seemed as if they had foster care services. Excited, feeling that I was on the verge of a new adventure, I called them both . . . and I was completely disappointed. One agency had a recorded message and I was able only to leave my name and address. The other had someone who knew nothing about the process answering the phone, and I could only give her my name and address. After a month or so, one agency sent a flier mentioning a foster parent information session. I never received anything from the other. I decided that these disorganized, unresponsive agencies were not the partners with whom we wanted to embark on a long-term relationship. I was excited and I wanted to work with people who would share my enthusiasm. A friend mentioned an agency in Manhattan that she had been dealing with on the adoption side; based on her positive experience, she suggested I call their foster care division. I called; they answered the phone; they mailed some materials. We chose to begin the process with them.

On January 25, fifteen days after my thirty-fourth birthday, ten days after we closed on our first house purchase, and four nights before Michael and I went to a law-firm dinner celebrating his election to partnership, I went to the Manhattan agency for an introductory session on becoming foster parents. The room was so full of people, the agency staff had to keep finding more chairs, so the session started late. The staff member who made the presentation asked how many people were interested in adopting. This surprised me because I hadn't given much thought to foster care as a route to adoption. I vaguely knew that this could happen, but I thought we were all there to become temporary caretakers. I was fascinated by the people around me, wondering what their motivations were for becoming foster parents. There were husband-and-wife teams, mother-and-daughter teams, single people—white, black, and Hispanic. There were not many suits and ties, but the room struck me as full of ordinary people, not the maladjusted, "in it for the money" types frequently portrayed in the media in the occasional foster care scandal. We left the session with green folders that contained an application and information about the foster parent certification process. The pamphlet at the front of the folder had a straightforward message on its cover: "Become a Foster Parent . . . Help a Child." That is exactly what Michael and I wanted to do.

The application asked about our current family, our own upbringing—including how we were disciplined (people who were abused as children are at higher risk of abusing their own children)—why we wanted to become foster parents, proof of our income and itemized monthly expenses, the number of children we would like to take, and the parameters of the conditions under which we would take a child, that is, race, sex, age, and emotional or physical handicaps. It was kind of fun to consider the implications of all the parameters; we agreed that we would take in one child, of either sex and any race, from birth to two years and would consider any handicap. I felt a little awkward about asking three people to send in letters of recommendation on our behalf, as required, because we were only in the initial stages of this process and I didn't want to publicize our intention in case we changed our minds. The contrast with having a biological child was remarkable in terms of how much simpler that process is and how much more private. When we decided to have our first baby, Michael and I had numerous discussions beforehand—and that was it. We didn't ask anyone if they thought we were ready or would be good parents or could support a child. And once I was pregnant, the process was passive. We didn't have to continue to fill out forms, get to various appointments and trainings, and make decisions. That blue-eyed boy whom we later discovered to be dyslexic grew in my belly without any further discussion on his father's and my part.

We were contacted for an interview that was scheduled for March 25. Many parts of the certification process felt invasive, as perfect strangers evaluated our ability to care for children with whom we had no biological ties. The foster parent certification process felt removed from what we would be expected to do in caring for children. It seemed to focus on keeping bad foster parents out, not necessarily getting good ones certified. For example, the purpose of looking at our monthly expenses was to ensure that we could support ourselves and weren't going to be looking for income to the monthly stipend meant to cover the child's expenses. Of course, this didn't guarantee that we would be good foster parents, that we would use the stipend to provide nutritious meals and serve them regularly just because we could afford to. I wanted somehow to be evaluated on my parenting ability. I'd think: Look at our two kids, they are happy and healthy. Or give me a test on child development. Let me show you that I am qualified to do this job.

Everyone at our agency was friendly and professional, but the scrutiny got to me at certain points and made me feel self-conscious. Even small things could seem significant. I evaluated our clothes before the interview. Were they clean and unwrinkled? Should we dress casually to show we were relaxed or dress up to indicate we thought the interview was important? I remember walking into the interview with Michael and Martha, the latter who was eating an apple, and I thought, They will see that we value good nutrition.

The interview was conducted by a social worker, a white woman we had met before who came across as experienced and professional, and by a psychologist, a white male. They reviewed the material on our application and we spent some time on practical concerns. We talked about how we would feel about getting up at night if we got a newborn after years of being able to sleep through the night. They seemed to have a hard time believing that we (I) didn't mind this. The social worker suggested that we change the earliest age that we would accept a child from birth to six months. "No, no," we assured her, "we love the early months." They asked how we would handle all the child care, as Michael works long hours and occasionally has to travel. This worried me as well. I had always been the primary caretaker for our children, but with the addition of a third child, I vowed to get some help so I could continue with my professional interests. After the interview, we were told that we could continue on to the training.

We attended two evening training sessions in April at the agency. Michael and I found that the most useful part of the training was meeting other prospective foster parents. The helpfulness of connecting to these other prospective parents reminded me of a class I had taken with Professor Alex Gitterman at Columbia. Alex, as he preferred to be called, is well known for his work with mutual aid groups, and one of the processes he spoke about in reference to these groups was the "all-in-the-same-boat phenomenon." This refers simply to the sharing of "mutual experience of ideas and emotions." When meeting other prospective foster parents, we felt relieved to see they had some of the same concerns and anxieties we had: What were relationships like between foster parents and birth parents? What were our obligations to the birth parents? How soon would a child be placed with us? How long would a child stay?

In our first session, we introduced ourselves, indicated whether we had children or not, and talked about what type of children we were interested in fostering. Some people were going through the training to be certified in kinship care, which allows a foster parent to take care of a family member's children. Others went through the training with a certain child in mind with whom they already had some tie. The rest were like us—open to whoever was in need—although while we preferred an infant, others (particularly those who worked full time) wanted school-age children. There was one Hispanic woman who twenty years ago had taken in and adopted a child who was deaf. Her son was now attending Gallaudet University, and she was interested in a second child. She stood out compared to the rest of the group because she was very professionally dressed.

The training included sections on child abuse and neglect—how to recognize the symptoms and how these may manifest in different aged children. There was a section on discipline that would be pretty straightforward if you already had children and had experimented with ways to discipline but would be helpful if you didn't. Some of the punishments that were listed as prohibited horrified me—one that comes to mind is forcing a child to kneel on rice. We were informed that all corporal punishment is prohibited by law for children in foster care.

We broke up into small groups and were given hypothetical discipline situations, which we then discussed how we would handle, and as Michael and I rode home on the subway, he showed me the problem his group was given to solve. A fifteen-year-old boy who had been in care with the foster parents for several months went to a baseball game and came home thirty minutes late, smelling of alcohol. The group's resolution was written in Michael's handwriting underneath the problem: "We would first make sure that Leon is physically okay, and ask him what and how much he had drunk. We would then ask Leon who he had been with, and why he had stayed out late and been drinking. We would tell Leon he is not allowed to go out with his friends for a week."

On the subway we talked about which of the other people we would choose for parents if we were children in foster care. Michael chose the woman whose son was deaf because he liked the compassion and pride in her voice when she referred to her son. I preferred another Hispanic woman who was a little older and overweight. She was warm and friendly and seemed comfortable with herself. We also spoke about how we felt better educated than some of the other prospective foster parents. I asked Michael what made him feel that way and he said that any time the group needed something read aloud, it seemed to fall to him. I had had the same experience in my group.

The training in April was followed by a home visit in May. The caseworker walked through our house looking for child guards on the windows and for smoke detectors. I felt like a real estate agent pushing a sale. She wanted to see the space where a child would sleep. I said, "Well, if it's a newborn, we'll keep it in our room. If it's a girl and two years old, she might sleep in Martha's room. If it's a boy . . . ," and so forth. She informed me that regulations prevent children over three years old from sleeping in the same room as a child of the opposite sex. I assumed this regulation was to prevent sexual abuse, and again I was shocked by the reality of some children's lives. Of course, during my MSW internships, I had contact with families where children had histories of abuse or neglect and it was always upsetting. But this felt different—I (and my family) would be getting to know a child on a very personal level in our own home.

We spoke about our decision to become foster parents with

the caseworker, and she asked Peter and Martha about their feelings in private. I wondered what they said, but they were both enthusiastic when talking to Michael and me so I assumed it was more of the same. Their one complaint to us was that the process took too long. The caseworker also spoke privately to two neighbors. Our home-study summary stated that we were "an educated, professional couple who have family and financial stability, . . . a couple who leads a lifestyle centered around the activities and needs of their children." However, three possible "problem" areas were identified: accommodating our busy lifestyles to the "appointments and regulations involved in foster parenting"; the appearance that we would attach easily to a child and the difficulty this could create for us, our children, and the child in care; and our ability to provide "financial resources that a child might not be accustomed to . . . and the resentment this could create for birth families."

And so with the approval of the agency as an acceptable foster family, we moved on to the final steps necessary for certification: fingerprinting, the child-abuse clearance check, and full medicals for the entire family. After receiving the jab for the TB test, Peter inquired if becoming a foster family would require any more "shots."

Michael and I were surprised at the deliberateness of the certification process and the effort it required of us. At times, we questioned whether it was worth it. However, as was true for any other tedious, bureaucratic process that we had gone through, once we finished, we rarely gave it a thought. In retrospect, some of our feelings about the process were probably tied up with our anxiety about doing something totally new to us. We were old enough and had enough parenting experience to know that this was going to be a life-changing event, and that was a bit frightening.

The entire process was pretty much complete by the beginning of the summer, six months after we began, but because I had one last semester of field placement to complete in the fall, we told the agency we wouldn't be ready for a child until December. However, in our enthusiasm, we offered to do short-term foster care during the summer. We were told that there wasn't much need for it, and we were called on only once, to take two-year-old twin boys for a week while their foster parents were on vacation. I contemplated the idea with fascination (twins had always seemed the ultimate parental challenge) and horror (two-year-olds!). Unfortunately, we couldn't take them because we were going on vacation the same week.

I started my field placement in September at a prevention program funded by New York City's Administration for Children's Services (ACS). Prevention programs are part of a new thrust to keep children out of foster care when possible. Not only is foster care very expensive, but also the forced separation is devastating and stigmatizing to children and their parents. Prevention programs help parents whose children are at risk of foster care placement through parenting classes and counseling and drug or alcohol rehabilitation, as well as give referrals for concrete services such as day care, educational programs, and housing. In cases where abuse and neglect are so severe that children need to be in foster care for their own safety, prevention programs wouldn't be appropriate.

The program I worked in seemed to provide a high level of service to the clients—the caseworkers, who all had master's degrees in social work, had small caseloads so that they could work intensively with their clients, with contact every week either in the client's home or in the office. The social workers were dedicated, and because the work was long term (up to two years), they became very attached to the families they worked with. On the few occasions when a client's children were put in foster care, I was struck by the social workers' anguish. They seemed heartbroken on behalf of these parents who were struggling, and personally disappointed that their own work wasn't more effective. When reading files and meeting clients, I was overwhelmed by their stories, which almost always included poverty, little education, few family or social supports (or at least not positive ones), and often a history of being sexually assaulted.

I finished this internship in December, and Michael and I put ourselves on the list to be called for a foster care placement on the fifteenth of that month. While excited about our new venture, I also felt somewhat predatory, waiting for another parent to stumble so we could pick up the pieces. I felt that I knew too much—these birth parents weren't evil monsters (or most of them anyway), they were unlucky people who had difficult lives. I also knew that children almost always want to be with the parents they know, regardless of how they are treated. I wrestled with my ambivalence. What is really best for these children? How bad do parents have to be to justify taking their children away?

At the same time, I spent the week before and after the fifteenth fantasizing about the fun we would have with another child around for the holidays. Michael had time off from work and it all seemed perfect. After two weeks of waiting, I stopped thinking about the possibility every time the phone rang. When we got a call on the thirtieth of December saying that the agency had a six-month-old Hispanic boy needing a placement, my heart began to race. When I ran up the stairs to ask Michael what he thought—he was shaving, as we planned to go out to dinner to celebrate our eleventh wedding anniversary that night—he thought I was joking. After a quick conference, we agreed to take the baby and waited for the call back. The caseworker called back to say that somebody else was already approved to take the child. She explained that ACS often calls several agencies in search of a placement and the first taker gets the child. Michael and I agreed: No more conferencing; the person who answers the phone makes the decision as to whether to accept the placement. I began to feel empathy for people who go through the adoption process.

Toward the end of February, Michael took a call from the agency at work asking us to take two siblings ages four and five. He declined, and we both felt guilty, even though we had agreed to accept a child only under the age of two. We felt that this would be a more natural and therefore easier transition for our two children, who are close in age and have a very tight relationship. We also felt better equipped to deal with the extra physical work of a small child versus the likelihood of emotional problems of an older child. Despite all our good reasons for not taking those children, we wondered about them and what would happen to them.

On Friday, later that week, I got another call from the agency asking if we would take a five-week-old girl who was African American. My heart began pounding and I said yes. The caseworker told me that we could get a call anytime over the weekend. I was perplexed that the timing could be so uncertain, but I didn't want to jeopardize the situation by asking any pesky questions. I called Michael and we spent most of Saturday making sure we were always available by telephone. We met Michael's brother and his wife, David and Sheila, for lunch in Greenwich Village, and we spoke in hushed tones about the baby's arrival so that Peter and Martha wouldn't hear, as we had chosen not to tell them until we were sure it would work out. It was the first time we were sharing our excitement publicly about a situation that seemed relatively concrete. We were actually somewhat certain that this little baby was coming to stay with us. David and Sheila, who had no children, not only welcomed our growing excitement, they joined in with us. They asked us questions, although we had little information to offer, and generally marveled with us at the uniqueness of the moment—our lives positioned to intersect with another's. At David's prompting, Michael kept checking his cell phone.

By Sunday, we were a little less charged, because we hadn't heard anything further. I went to Rite Aid anyway and bought diapers, bottles, and formula. I spent considerable time choosing the items, noting the technological improvements since Peter and Martha were infants. As I agonized over the cutest pacifier, I had flashbacks to my childhood, when with my Christmas money I bought real diapers and baby food for my dolls. When I showed my purchases to my oldest sister, Lynn, she explained the wastefulness of buying real baby food for a doll and returned the items to our corner grocery. (I think she let me keep the diapers.) I knew Lynn was right, but I had wanted to make my doll more real. I wasn't pregnant now; was this baby whom I had never met real?

On Monday, Michael had to go to Chicago for the night for a work meeting. At 9 AM, I called the agency and my contact there said she was quite sure this baby was going to come to us because her siblings were already in foster care. She informed me that when children have been taken away from the biological parent, ACS automatically investigates after the birth of a sibling to see if the family circumstances have improved and would permit adequate parenting. The circumstances of this birth mother hadn't changed and didn't seem likely to in the short term. The caseworker also told me that they thought the baby would move to another foster home in June to live with a half sister. She told me that since the agency was already handling the siblings, it would also supervise this baby's placement with a foster family. She said she would be back in touch. As I hung up, I realized I was already attaching to this child I had never met. Why was ACS taking so long to remove her if they felt she was unsafe with her mother?

I called my friend Karen, who had been a support throughout the application process and who had a two-year-old daughter. We had a good time sitting on her living room floor sorting through the baby things. "Oh, remember when Rachael wore this?" I'd say. "She looked so cute in it." Karen would say, "You have to take this sweater, my mother bought this for Leah. I love the pattern on it." She offered a bassinet, blankets, clothing, and a stroller. I took everything home in a cab and tucked it all away in my room so that the kids wouldn't see it when they got home from school.

At five o'clock, I got another call from the agency asking if we would take two Russian immigrant sisters, ages three and four, for a few months only. I was bewildered and said that I might consider it (because it was so short term) except that we had already agreed to take an infant. She paused and asked, "Who are you expecting?" When I told her the baby's family name, the caseworker said she thought that it would probably happen. Shortly after that phone call, Peter saw the bassinet in my room and started shouting, "Martha, Martha, we're going to get a baby!"

To help pass the time and because I didn't feel like making dinner, we accepted the invitation of another family to eat out at our favorite local Japanese restaurant, Inaka. Since the baby's arrival seemed so imminent, I shared our news. In fact, I could hardly sit still and at one point during dinner, I ran home two blocks and checked our answering machine to make sure I hadn't missed anything. Martha and Peter seemed quite relaxed, and Martha spent a lot of the dinner spelling her name out in bean pods while her friend Maeve did the same. To help share in our excitement, our friends treated us to dinner.

After I put the kids to bed, I spent some time on the phone talking to my mother, my sisters, and Michael's brother, who had all been on alert through the weekend and wanted to know the news. The conversations were short little snatches because I didn't want to tie up the telephone line. "No, I haven't heard anything. I'll call you back." At nine o'clock, a caseworker from ACS called to say that they had the baby and they were waiting for medical clearance. He thought they would arrive in a few hours.

2

And Baby Makes Five?

TUESDAY MORNING, I had to take the older kids to school, something Michael normally did that fell to me when he was traveling. The school is only about a ten-minute walk away—a pleasant walk, really. But that day, feeling a mixture of sleep deprivation and elation, I would have preferred to stay cocooned in my own house rather than face my neighbors and the February morning. It had been six years since I had cared for an infant and I had had less than twelve hours to get to know this one; I felt a bit nervous and self-conscious exposing us both to the outside world. However, I managed to get breakfast served, lunches made, and Cecilia bundled up in an old snowsuit of Peter's and snuggled into the stroller. Even the ordinary things I did felt special because I had this new life with me. I remember that day as one where I felt really alive, a day where I wouldn't have wanted to switch places with anyone because what was happening to my family and me seemed so extraordinary.

Pushing the stroller up the street toward the school, I had a flashback to my childhood. As a young girl, I had what felt to me a very lifelike baby doll. One day when I was six or seven, I was pushing the doll carriage up the street with my baby, Betsy, inside. An older woman neighbor stopped to admire my "baby." For a split second, it felt as if she had stepped into my imaginary world, as if she thought my doll was real.. That is how I felt thirty years later, pushing this new "doll" up the street: "Is this real or am I imagining it?"

Cecilia's sudden arrival made it obvious to those I knew that I had not given birth to this child, also apparent to anyone who saw the difference in our skin color. I felt extremely self-conscious about this. That first day the contrast between my pale skin and Cecilia's brown skin seemed glaring. Not only did I feel that I had someone else's child, I felt that I had a child from another culture. Would I owe someone an explanation?

While there had been plenty of anticipation and discussion within our family and among our close friends, we hadn't talked about the possibility of becoming foster parents much with others because the likelihood seemed so uncertain and so strange. Maybe part of our reluctance to announce our plans had to do with our anxiety—the fewer people we told, the easier it would be to change our minds. I also felt superstitious. When I was pregnant, I felt I could tell the world, because most likely I would deliver a baby—in any event, whether I miscarried or not, I *was* pregnant. In this case, a baby was more a plan than an actuality, and there were so many unknowns that I often felt I didn't know where to begin. We hadn't known the age or sex or circumstances of the child who would come to us. And perhaps most importantly, as we were told in the training, we would have no control over what would happen next—placement decisions were not made by the foster parents. I am a planner by nature, and planning is one of the ways I reduce my anxiety about new situations. In the years and especially the months before we actually became foster parents, I imagined what it would be like. What would my schedule be if I had a six-month-old or a two-year-old? Would I work part-time or full-time? Would we baby proof the house? Would some vacation still be manageable? Should I save the portacrib? And so on. And what if I found the child unlikable? What if he screamed through the night and we couldn't manage and we gave him back? It seemed better not to tell too many people, in case we failed. Or in case using words to describe what I expected would jinx me into a situation entirely different from my fantasy.

When I did have conversations out of necessity—with my next-door neighbor, Britta, for example, so that she could be interviewed as part of our application process—there was an awkwardness. One day, I caught up with Britta on the street in front of our adjoining houses as we both were coming home in the evening. "Hey," I said, "we're thinking about becoming foster parents."

"Oh, really?" She looked surprised.

"Yes. I was wondering if you wouldn't mind being interviewed on our behalf. You know, just to say that we are decent parents." I laughed nervously. "I hope, anyway."

"Of course," Britta replied. "When would you get a child?"

"I'm not really sure. Once we're certified as foster parents, we'll be put on a list and then we'll wait."

"Wow!" As she paused, I could see that she was processing what I had just said. Then she asked, "What age child would you take?"

"Well, we have said birth to two years—I'm not sure what age, exactly."

"How long will you have the child?"

I responded with forced confidence. "You really can't tell. It depends on the family circumstances. The agency has told me that we could expect a child to stay with us for a year."

Britta didn't say anything, but even I was thinking that a year is a really long time.

After depositing Peter and Martha in school that first morning, I paused outside where I had left the stroller in front of the steps. I stood with Cecilia in my arms, and a group of mothers gathered around me. I was a little overwhelmed. I was meeting some of these mothers for the first time; they were drawn to the little crowd by the excitement. As their eyes feasted on the baby, I didn't even wait for the inevitable questions. "This is Cecilia," I announced. "She is our foster daughter."

"Oh how wonderful!" the women all responded in chorus, some with tears welling in their eyes, making mine fill in return. "How long will you have her?" someone asked.

My answer was hesitant. "I'm not really sure—probably at least through June."

Another woman lamented, "Oh, you're going to get really attached."

The questions and comments stung a little because they got to the heart of my already emerging confusion about my foster parenting role. The models—social worker, babysitter, parent—that I was familiar with and that I thought would be relevant to help me in this new role didn't quite fit. Although I really cared about some of my past clients, I could live with ambiguity as a social worker because the clients didn't affect my life. While sometimes I had felt emotionally involved, more frequently I was thinking analytically. As for babysitting, I knew the expectations and the limits: You are a substitute caretaker, the parents make all the big decisions, and the responsibility is short term. I hadn't even met the mother of the child I was caring for; she was clearly not in charge. With parenting too, I understood the demands and the rewards. While the responsibility was tremendous, the bonds were deep and forever. Foster parenting was a form of child care that was unfamiliar to me. In short order, the complexity of the situation struck me. Clearly, I was the *temporary* caretaker, but I was in my own home and completely responsible for an infant so young that she had probably not formed attachments to her birth mother.

When we began the process to become foster parents and I imagined the whole process, I focused on my pleasure and my pride at the end of the placement. In a loosely imagined fantasy, I could see myself handing over a healthy child to a weary but capable (and maybe even grateful?) mother. I didn't think much about my own attachment to the child, because I didn't think of the child as belonging to me. I would like to think that I stopped short of viewing Michael and myself as heroes. But I certainly thought our role would make a difference, or else we never would have begun the process. The problem was that my scenario depended on returning the child to a capable family—and that, I now realized, was completely out of my control.

At home, the door closed to the cold and the outside world, I brought Cecilia up to my bedroom. Now that our secret was out and she was here, I could begin to incorporate her into our physical space. I began with the bedroom because that is the heart of daily life with an infant. I slipped her out of the snowsuit and laid her down in her cozy bassinet and began to arrange the diapers and clothes from Karen into a makeshift changing area at the end of my bed. When Cecilia fussed, I made up a bottle and fed her, watching her cheeks move as she happily sucked the formula down. She was a natural with the bottle. I held her snug in the crook of my arm in the rose-fabric-covered chaise lounge that Michael's stepmother had given us.

After the burping, Cecilia lay in my lap and I raised my knees so we could spend some time looking at one another. Rather than spring into my usual efficient morning routine—making my bed, then moving on to my list of chores or work—I lounged. The bed stayed rumpled and the chores undone as I moved in time with the natural rhythms of a small baby—eat, sleep, change, admire, and so on. I've read somewhere that something in breast milk relaxes a new mother, but I think the weight and warmth and tininess of an infant alone can slow your life down to a pleasant and peaceful pace.

When later that morning I looked through the few items in a plastic bag that had been left with Cecilia, I separated out the clothes I wanted to give away, and I felt guilty: ACS had stripped them off her the night before, and here I was getting rid of them. I didn't want to think about where the clothes came from, and I knew that every time I saw them, I would think about Cecilia's mother, and that made me uncomfortable. I knew I would look at those clothes and my eyes would focus on the "12 months" tag in the back of the white turtleneck and red jumpsuit with little trucks on it and I would wonder where her mother got the clothes and why they were so big. Not that there is anything wrong with wrapping a five-week-old in twelve-month clothes. It's all just fabric, after all. But I knew I would think about the diapers and blankets and snowsuits that a baby needs and wonder if Cecilia's mother had access to these things. Elements of my good foster parent intentions were breaking down already as I questioned whether giving away the clothes that the birth mother had put on her daughter just the day before indicated my less than whole-hearted support.

I also got rid of the baby bottle that still held some formula. I considered trying to scrub the spoiled formula out of the bottle so we could keep something of Cecilia's early life and decided that with such a small baby it was better to weigh in on the side of caution and make sure all the bottles were sanitary. But something about the bottle caught my attention. It might have been the "I Love my Mommy" written on the side, but it was also the formula. I stared at it as if it were some clue to a mystery. If I had access to a lab, I could have had the contents analyzed: What time yesterday did this baby's mother make up her last bottle? In the end, I saved only a pair of socks from the bag. I put them in a special drawer in my dresser where I keep the sweaters that my sister Audrey made for Martha when she was an infant and where I have some white leather gloves from my great-grandmother.

While some new parents might feel that their expectations had not come close to the reality of having an infant (especially particularly difficult infants), this had never been a problem for me. I had lots of experience with children before giving birth to Peter and Martha, and I felt well prepared and confident when they arrived. But with Cecilia, I began to feel unnerved by some of the unnatural emotional aspects of my maternal role.

That first day, a legal aid lawyer called and introduced herself as the law guardian for Cecilia. She gave me her name and telephone number and asked me if we were "preadoptive." I said no, but I was mystified by her question, as I had thought the plan was eventually to reunify the baby with her mother. I had been told that Cecilia was to be placed with an older half sister in her foster home in June, when a young boy living there was due to be reunified with his mother. Our conversation was short because I didn't know enough to ask questions. I didn't understand the lawyer's role. The term "law guardian" implied that she was an advocate for Cecilia's legal rights. What rights did a five-week-old have? How did the law-guardian role differ from the agency role? How did this stranger know what was best for Cecilia?

The question of whether we were preadoptive lingered in my mind over the next weeks and months. It also confirmed for me that my confusion over my role was justified. Clearly we were considered an option as permanent caretakers. I was relieved that we ourselves were confident that we were going to do only short-term foster care, and I could answer the legal guardian's question with certainty and not confuse myself further. And I tried not to think too much about the plan for Cecilia. She had lived with her mother for five weeks; she would live with us for four months; and then she would live with another foster mother, who would either return her to her birth mother or adopt her. Thinking too clearly about that plan would have overwhelmed me, as it was contrary to what I intuitively felt as a mother. In their first year of life, Michael and I probably left Peter and Martha with caretakers fewer than five times.

Later that afternoon, I had to take Cecilia with me to class, my final course to complete my degree, as I had nowhere to leave her on such short notice. I packed my bag with my notebook and folder, but I was less certain what to bring for the baby. She had been with me less than twenty-four hours and there was still so much I didn't know about her. So I brought everything: extra outfits (Does this baby spit up a lot?); bottles with formula (I packed enough for a one-year-old—the last thing I wanted was a starving, shrieking five-week-old on the subway or in class); diapers and wipes; a pacifier (Would she use one?); and a blanket for the unlikely event that she spit up on all the clothing and I had nothing left to put her in, which happened to me once when Peter was an infant. I put Cecilia in the Snugli—I was nervous about whether I would be able to manage the stroller on the subway by myself, and Cecilia, at five weeks and only eight pounds eleven ounces, seemed so vulnerable and small, I felt I should keep her close.

I took the #2 train to the Upper West Side and Columbia. I sat with the baby, trying to read my *New Yorker*, but I was unable to focus. No one was staring at me, but I felt they should be: I was a white woman with a black infant. I thought I remembered from one of my classes that the National Association of Black Social Workers (NABSW) was against transracial placements. In my highly charged emotional state, I wondered if someone might confront me, might say, "What are you doing with that baby?"

I also had the sense that people might be staring at me because my feeling that my life had changed seemed so palpable. It didn't seem unreasonable to imagine that strangers would be able to see the difference. "Look at me—my life has changed. I have someone else's baby." I felt the same way I did in eighth grade when my mother gave me a ring with a small sapphire and diamond chips in it for my birthday; my great-grandfather had given it to her when she turned thirteen. I remember being on the bus on the way home from school, surrounded by adolescents, and thinking how odd that they couldn't see how I had changed, how I was more adult.

My class was the second half of a yearlong research project in which a small group of students took on a proposal from an outside agency, conducted research, and tried to write a publishable article. My group looked at a mentoring program developed by a foster care agency: Parents who had gotten their children out of foster care acted as mentors to birth parents who were still trying to straighten out their lives and get their children back. Mentor support can be crucial for these parents, because by the time they lose their children to foster care, their lives are often in such a deteriorated state that they have little, if any, positive support among family or in their community.

One of the reasons that evaluating this program was especially timely was that the Adoption and Safe Families Act of 1997 required states to initiate termination of parental rights for parents of children who had been in foster care for fifteen of the most recent twenty-two months. Previous legislation had required extensive family-reunification efforts. Unfortunately, the effect of this process on too many children had been long-term foster care, which could be very damaging. The new legislation was an attempt to help children find alternative permanent families more quickly if they could not return to their birth families.

Cecilia's presence in class caused quite a stir. Nervous about what the other students and the professors would think or say, I made a beeline for the front left corner of the room, where I usually sat. Schools of social work can be very political places, with many students who have lots of energy but little life experience taking up crusades on behalf of people who have had a hard time speaking up for themselves. Birth mothers with children in foster care were one group that fell in this category. I hadn't made it halfway across the room when a student said, "Hey, you have a baby!" Students got up from their seats and gathered around me, Cecilia still tied to my chest. I had never seen the class so animated; it felt as if we were at a small party. Most of the other students did not have children and were fascinated with such a small baby. The professor and our teaching assistant took turns admiring her, and I could see the flicker that crosses the minds of most women who have had children and see a newborn—the sight takes you back. After half an hour of cooing and holding, the professor announced, "All right, back to work."

Our small group of five assembled, taking turns holding the baby while the others worked diligently to input data. As part of the project, we compiled statistics on 123 birth parents. While we worked, I was struck by the scene—the stale, stuffy computer room animated by the freshness of a newborn whose mother could fit the profile of one of the women in our project. While some data were missing from our surveys, the information we did gather indicated that the overwhelming majority of birth parents belonged to minority groups; 58 percent of those who were working to get their children back were African American and 31 percent were Hispanic. Unsurprisingly, they were also mostly women—82 percent. And these parents were poorly educated, as well; 48 percent did not finish high school and an additional 44 percent had no education beyond high school or a GED certificate. Fifty-nine percent had their children placed in foster care due to neglect. And substance abuse was an issue for at least 41 percent of the birth parents. Our research showed that our figures were not out of line with statistics on birth parents for all of New York City.

To support our quantitative data and to better understand the parents we would be interviewing for the second part of our project, we read many articles on child abuse and neglect. Child-maltreatment researcher Jay Belsky argues that "there is no one pathway to these disturbances in parenting; rather, maltreatment seems to arise when stressors outweigh supports and risks are greater than protective factors" (1993, 427). Three risks he mentions are youth, poverty, and lack of education. Another social work researcher, Martha Dore, illustrates the vulnerability of some families to child maltreatment with the diagram shown in Figure 1.

When I spoke to Wendy, a doctoral student and the teaching assistant for our project, during the class, she asked me what the plan was for reunification of Cecilia with her family. I told her that I hadn't been given all the details but in the short term, the

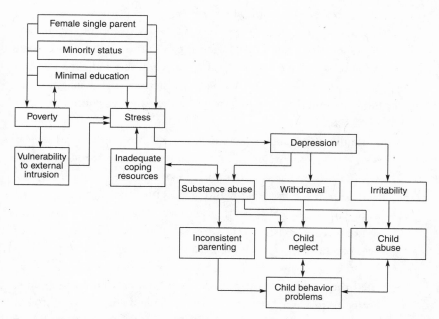

Figure 1. Pathways to child maltreatment in poor families. Reprinted by permission from Dore 1993, fig. 1.1.

plan was for her to move to another foster home to live with a half sister. Wendy rested her eyes on Cecilia and remarked, "She's awfully sweet."

"I know," I replied. "It makes you feel like you are preying on these parents somehow."

"Well, you are," Wendy replied, not unkindly.

That night Michael rushed home from work to meet Cecilia. He was desperate to see her, particularly after having missed out on the excitement of her arrival. He picked her up immediately and spent some time with her while intercepting excited questions and comments from Peter and Martha. He held Cecilia's small body in his big hands against his chest, bouncing her lightly and rhythmically.

I said, "You probably don't need to do that. She really isn't fussy."

He replied, "All babies love this."

Michael put aside his usual evening work so we could take care of the kids together. Rather than the hesitation that he had when Peter was first born—for example, "Can you help me change his diaper?"—Michael snapped into action with Cecilia, skillfully changing and feeding her. I marveled at his confidence and enthusiasm.

I didn't think about how much more comfortable it was to deal with the sociodemographic characteristics of a parent on paper, as I had in my class, rather with than the parent herself, until I learned that the first visit with Cecilia's birth family would be the next day, Wednesday, from 5:00–7:00 PM. The New York State standard is one visit every two weeks, but in a sincere effort to help parents reunify with their children, our agency required visits every week. I thought about my older two children as I calculated the two-hour visit plus the two-hour traveling time—four hours every week for which I would have to find a babysitter. I also felt trepidation. I spent a lot of time thinking about how I would feel if my child was taken from me and wondered about the scene where Cecilia was taken from her mother. I imagined crying, screaming. I assumed that her mother would be angry, and I was worried that she would direct her anger at me. This all felt overdramatic, but I had no way of knowing how her experiences would influence her feelings. I could only imagine how I would feel—my feelings as a result of my own experiences as a child and as a parent now.

To get to the visit, I took the F train from Brooklyn to Manhattan with Cecilia in the Snugli. The midtown location seemed an odd one for a social service agency, since the area is mostly office buildings and shops. The agency was located on the third floor of a nice office building, but as soon as the doors of the elevator opened onto the third floor, the formal office environment evaporated. That evening, the waiting room was teeming with birth and foster parents, the children everywhere.

I arrived ahead of Cecilia's birth mother and met the social worker in the waiting room. She was pleasant—typical of most of the social workers we would have—young, female, white, and hard-working. I had a thousand questions but found it difficult to articulate them: Who is this baby? Where does she come from? How do I fit in this picture? Should I be in this picture? The situation was so unlike any other I had ever been in, I was at a loss for words. I didn't want to ask anything intrusive or inappropriate, but I didn't know what questions would fall into those categories in these circumstances. The one question I mustered was, "What is the mom like?" The answer: "She doesn't say too much, actually." I had learned in a previous conversation that Cecilia's mother was mildly retarded, that she lived in a shelter, and that Cecilia was the youngest of her five daughters. The oldest daughter, Sierra*, was six, the same age as Martha, and she lived with her paternal grandfather. The second two were Brittney and MaryKate, ages

---

* Most names in this book and a few identifying details have been changed for privacy reasons.

three and four. They lived together in a foster home in the Bronx. The fourth daughter, Dawn, was one year old, and she lived in another foster home in the Bronx. This was the sister Cecilia was scheduled to join in June. Cecilia did not share a father with any of the other girls. The agency did not know the whereabouts of Cecilia's father.

The Foster Care System

I sat next to the social worker with my eyes focused on the elevators, my heart beating rapidly. I wondered how I would recognize Cecilia's mother, but when the doors opened on a tall, dark-complexioned woman in a brown leather vest, she made a beeline for me. She seemed upset, and I couldn't turn Cecilia over to her fast enough. I don't recall if we even spoke to each other. After Cecilia and her mother headed down a hallway to have their visit in another room, I was told that the foster parents usually hand off the children to the parents and the social workers monitor the visits. So I went to a nearby cafe and did some schoolwork. It was hard to concentrate; I wondered how the reunion was going. But I appreciated the time to myself—usually I would be home making dinner at that hour. When I picked Cecilia up at seven o'clock, she seemed oblivious to the shift in caretakers and her mother was visibly more relaxed, even as she handed the baby to me to bundle up and take home.

The first visit was stressful for me, not because of any interactions with the baby's family but because of my discomfort with the situation. I continued to wrestle with my feelings about what circumstances could justify removing a child from her birth family, although of course I had no say in the matter. It was hard to separate from my social worker self and just be a foster parent. As a social worker, it was easy for me to empathize with the birth mother; as a foster parent, it was much more difficult because I had *her* child. It seemed to me that I was profiting in some way from the situation, and it would have been much easier just to dislike the birth mother, look down on her, find any excuse to justify the circumstances.

The complexity of my relationship with Cecilia's birth mother seemed influenced by how it all began. Cecilia was dropped off to me in the middle of the night in mysterious circumstances, reminiscent of some modern-day stork. I met Cecilia and began to know her completely separate from any of her birth family. I wondered whether, if I had met the birth mom first and she had given me her infant directly, the relationship would have felt different. As it was, foster mother (me) meets child and then meets birth mother. It should have been birth mother meets another mother (me) and (temporarily) gives me her child.

The transitional period was intense over the first weeks and slowly settled down over the following several months. The move from two children to three was exciting and stimulating. All our close friends and family were excited. Michael's colleagues sent baby clothes and good wishes. We felt supported; many friends and family members gave us gifts for the baby as well as second-hand clothing and baby equipment. Michael's brother, David, and his wife, Sheila, brought us a beautiful bunch of pale pink tulips. The first weekend, my sister Natalie and her family, who lived in Connecticut, met us at a rest stop on the New York State Thruway as we were en route upstate. They wanted to meet the baby. At lunch inside the rest stop, Natalie and Mark and my nephews admired and held Cecilia. Afterward, Natalie moved her car into the parking spot right next to our station wagon so that we could transfer from her trunk to ours the changing table, stroller, clothes, and toys they had brought.

Despite all the good wishes and support, sometimes the lack of ritual and uncertainty filtered through. Part of the difficulty lay in our continued efforts to define our roles as foster parents. For those in our community, the sudden, unusual, and transitory nature of our changed family situation was often uncomfortable.

The baby came into our mostly white, upper-middle-class world without the usual cultural rituals—anticipation, baby announcements, baby shower, and so on. It bothered me that Cecilia didn't have the same fanfare other children had when they were born or adopted. Why does it matter? I thought. She doesn't know any different. But ritual is part of our human social condition and not being able to partake in it on her behalf made me unhappy.

In the meantime, I did what I could by taking pictures and starting a photo album of Cecilia's first year. I also spent a lot of time searching for a baby book in which I could record all her precious baby facts so that nothing would be lost. When this baby went to her forever family, I wanted her and the family to have all the pieces of her life.

Brenda Smith, an Australian social worker, has written that in her country, "the majority of foster children come from the most socially disadvantaged and stigmatized families, particularly those headed by mothers, and are mostly cared for by upper-working-class foster mothers and supervised by middle-class welfare workers" (Smith 1991, 175–76). This is true too in the United States, where except via the professional roles of lawyers or social workers, foster care rarely touches the middle class. The first time I took Cecilia into the agency medical office, the doctor asked what my husband and I did for a living. She then asked why we chose to become foster parents. The real curiosity in her voice made it obvious how unusual we were.

The people I know who can't or choose not to have birth children have adopted through domestic private adoptions or internationally, at a cost of $15,000 to $30,000. The majority of children in foster care are placed with and sometimes eventually adopted by working-class people in their own neighborhoods (Sengupta 2000). A conundrum that would nag at me over the next months was why middle-class Americans showed little to no interest in these children (aside from shaking their collective heads at the occasional horror story in the media) but could go to so much trouble and expense for children from other countries. I wondered if it was race, class, the bureaucracy, the stigma of U.S. foster care, or the excitement of a foreign nation, language, and culture? Ignorance? The discomfort of being too close to the reality of the birth child's family?

It is hard to discern the cause of this phenomenon, which involves such complex and emotional issues. Of course, many people are simply desperate to adopt, and it is understandably appealing to them to go to poverty-stricken countries and adopt young children where there is virtually no chance of ever having contact with the birth family. Distance and race must also have something to do with it, as there are healthy African American infants who are adopted by Australians and Canadians each year. However, others adopt for humanitarian reasons—something I have considered, as it is so hard to read about the intense suffering of other people, especially children. Why don't these people ever become foster parents or adopt one of the thousands of children in foster care who are already freed for adoption in the United States? Then they could send the thousands of dollars they would save to other countries to aid many children instead of just one.

Our decision to become foster parents forced people in our community to think about what happens to a child after she has been removed from her home. It wasn't always comfortable territory. One day, I was out with Cecilia in the stroller on Seventh Avenue, our main shopping street. A block away, I could see Meredith, from my book group, coming toward me. While I had attended this book group for two years, I had never felt a close part of the group, which seemed to have meshed years before I joined. So I was no more than a casual friend to Meredith. As I approached, I could see her staring at me and the stroller. In the awkward pause after our greetings, I said, "We have become foster parents."

"Really?" she responded with a confused but curious expression. "Wow, how old is she?"

"Six weeks," I said with a smile.

"How long will you have her?"

I stiffened in anticipation of the "list of most-asked questions" but replied, "Probably through June."

"What happened to her mother?" (No one ever asked about Cecilia's father.) "Does she have siblings?"

Meredith's raw curiosity felt so different from times when the curiosity was mixed with genuine concern and support. My friend Susan, for instance, said, referring to the baby's eventual departure, "It will be difficult, but you are a strong family, you will be able to handle it."

I found people's comments generally fell into two categories. The surprised, "Oh, how wonderful!" response covered most of them. Some said they were impressed we were actually doing something that many people only think about. When I heard this, it made me feel powerful that we were using our lives in a meaningful way. I had conversations with women in which we discussed what I found to be the surprisingly common fantasy of a baby left on the doorstep. The number of people who had thought about caring for a child that they hadn't adopted or given birth to amazed me. I had never had these conversations before, but somehow our actions made it safe for people to expose these thoughts.

In the second category were the more infrequent but more painful responses often said in voices filled with anxiety and uncertainty. "How are you ever going to handle this? I could never do that, I would get too attached." I answered that question which had no answer lamely and with an uncomfortable smile. I often felt angry that people I hardly knew asked me such personal questions. Partly it seemed an invasion of our privacy, but partly it probed feelings we were uncomfortable with.

I spent time thinking of "appropriate" responses (most of which weren't very nice). Sometimes I would detail these encounters to Michael at night in the privacy of our bedroom. "The next time someone tells me that they would get too attached," I'd tell him, "I'm going to say, 'You're probably right. Why bother risking your own feelings for a kid you don't even know? I mean, really, who cares?'" The conversations we had on this topic helped me immensely with my own feelings. Michael knew exactly what I was talking about and what I was feeling, as he too had these encounters. And, as with our instincts on parenting, we generally had the same reactions to these situations. We talked about how warnings about "getting too attached" sometimes seemed to imply the speaker was taking the high road—suggesting how sensitive they were when in fact they probably didn't want to disrupt their lives, a more honest and understandable excuse. We wanted to say to people, "Yes, getting attached is a risk, but we are adults and we are supposed to care about children in our society, even if it is difficult."

In our culture, people do not ask parents who aren't close friends personal probing questions about their attachment to their children or about their family members who have problems with alcohol, for example. In our experience this reticence did not extend to children in foster care. One time, Michael and I were in the skate shop close to our house buying ice skates with the kids. We ran into a neighborhood acquaintance who seemed to be having a particularly difficult time with our situation. In front of our children, as she had done on several previous occasions, she asked about the update on Cecilia's situation and how we were dealing with it. Michael's responses were terse. When her daughters came over to us, she abruptly changed the subject. She seemed to feel that *her* children were too precious to hear the difficult details that she so enjoyed trying to extract from us.

I continually felt grateful that Cecilia was a baby, oblivious to all the discomfort around her. I didn't think I was strong enough to shoulder my own emotions as well as those of a child old enough to be aware of her precarious circumstances. But Martha and Peter were old enough, and they were not oblivious to the commentary. It made them uncomfortable, and I regret that I wasn't able sooner to find a polite way to say, "Mind your own business." I was also grateful that Michael and I were of like mind as we weathered the stress of this initial transition period. After all, I was the one who had pushed us to become foster parents, and I occasionally feared that Michael might suddenly feel overwhelmed or regretful.

While I did fleetingly worry about Michael's commitment, we worked as a team caring for Cecilia. When we were going through the foster application process, Michael said that he could not spare any work time to care for a child, although he would pitch in equally when he was home. However, when I took a friend to a show to celebrate her birthday one afternoon in March just a few weeks after Cecilia had come to us, I had barely mentioned that I didn't know who would care for the baby when Michael volunteered that he could meet me in midtown Manhattan for a few hours in the middle of his workday. When we met up after the show, it was unclear to me who had enjoyed the time the most, me watching the musical or Michael getting coffee and hanging out with the baby. Michael enjoyed caring for Cecilia, and he had the confidence to do so from our experiences parenting Peter and Martha.

It was a relief when I encountered someone who knew something about or had experience with foster care. The first time I took Martha to her weekly gymnastics class with Cecilia in tow, the woman at the front desk who answered the phone and took attendance, and whom I knew only casually, asked about the baby in the stroller. I explained that we had become foster parents. She replied that her parents also took in a child from foster care. She then added simply, "He is my brother—we adopted him." We exchanged smiles. A teacher at the kids' school shared with me that her mother had been a foster parent. Our brief conversation about her mother's experience was helpful to me.

Because foster care is an institution so far removed from the middle class, I found myself on the receiving end of countless questions about why children enter foster care. Most often, I was asked specifically why Cecilia entered care, but I felt most comfortable responding with my "social worker self" about why children in general come into care. For one thing, the agency had told us not to share specific details about Cecilia's history. For another, I preferred to educate people rather than feed their curiosity, even though I don't feel that any details of Cecilia's life are shameful. I would tell people that children are removed from their homes either because they were neglected and/or abused physically, sexually, or emotionally. I would say that most cases are complicated by many other factors that contribute to the abuse and/or neglect, such as domestic violence, lack of housing (although this cannot be the sole reason for removing a child from the parent), substance abuse, poor parenting skills, and poverty.

Most children removed from their birth families are victims of neglect. This can mean that they are not fed or clothed adequately, do not get proper medical care, do not attend school, or are left unsupervised at a young age. Interestingly, there is no law in New York State that spells out at what age a child is old enough to be left home alone—most situations depend on the circumstances, such as the age/maturity of the child and the length of time the child is left alone. While this makes some sense, it also leaves parents more vulnerable to someone else's judgment call, especially those already receiving social service benefits. For example, a doctor in a public health clinic with whom the parent has no relationship is more likely to report child abuse or neglect than another parent's private pediatrician, whose children might even go to school together.

There is no question that poverty is related to abuse and neglect, although exactly how remains unclear. The confluence of factors that determines how situations of possible abuse or neglect are interpreted, reported, and acted upon surely includes race and class. A statistic makes this painfully clear: In 1998, in families with incomes below $10,000 who lived in Central Harlem (a predominantly black and poor area of Manhattan), 120 per 1,000 children were put in foster care. Less than a mile away, in families on the Upper East Side (a wealthy, predominantly white area of Manhattan) whose incomes were also below $10,000, only 4 children per 1,000 were placed in foster care (*Community Data Profiles* 1998).

Michael and I had been planning for a year to spend five days in March with my sister Lynn and our brother-in-law Max, who were Fulbright scholars in Budapest. The trip would be a welcome respite from our household responsibilities, as Peter and Martha would visit their maternal and paternal grandparents in Albany while we were gone. Cecilia arrived three weeks before our scheduled departure date, but we never considered canceling the trip, although we did briefly wonder whether the addition of an infant would ruin the fun. Still, no matter how tenuous our bond to this new child, our instincts as parents were strong. Besides, my sister wanted to meet her, and I wanted to see my sister and brother-in-law, whom I missed. We hadn't chosen to be foster parents so we could put our lives on hold; the plan was to incorporate the child into our lives.

While I knew it would be best for Cecilia to stay with us, now her primary caretakers, I was unsure what the agency would say. As a social worker, I knew that there were different standards for one's own children and those in city care. Most social workers have so many children on their caseloads that they might not always make choices that would be best for the children—sometimes they take the easiest option and the one that follows the regulations most clearly. Necessity, which sprang from caseworkers being overworked and lacking resources, often bred a "good enough" attitude. However, the foster care agency readily agreed to get the birth mother's permission for the trip. It may have been easier to help me than to find another placement on short notice. The agency gave me a letter that explained our relationship as Cecilia's foster parents and gave us permission to take her out of the country.

In a rush, I made an appointment to get a passport for Cecilia three days before we were to leave, unprepared for the fifteen hours the process would demand. I took the #1 train back and forth between the passport office, where everyone was well informed and there were tidy lines for everything, and the city records office, where many of the clerks were gruff and poorly informed. The biggest challenge was trying to convince the city records office to give me a birth certificate with Cecilia's name on it, as her original birth certificate had "female" instead of her first name.

Friends told me I would never get the passport in time, but I became determined. I refused to even think about alternative plans. In her first eight weeks of life, Cecilia had already lived with two unrelated families. Consistent care is important for infants as they form attachments that will provide them with models for life. I knew this baby needed to be with us—I thought five days with strangers would be wrong (she had to be with licensed foster parents and therefore couldn't even stay with my mother). In an odd way, the ordeal seemed like a test of our commitment to Cecilia, and it was refreshing to feel so certain.

The day before we were to leave, in the second-to-last phase of my passport odyssey, I found myself sitting on a wooden bench among many arranged like church pews facing the passport agents' bullet-proof altar. I was doing embroidery to pass the time and

calm my nerves, but my hands were so sweaty from anxiety that
I had to keep wiping them on my pants because the needle was
slipping in my fingers. I was called up to speak with an agent, Ms.
Love. "Love," I thought to myself, "is a good sign." She wore a
bright orange sweater and radiated warmth. I explained the situation and gave her all my papers. After some faxing back and forth
to the foster care agency for more official documentation, she gave
me the okay for a one-year conditional passport. I felt like jumping over the counter and hugging her.

I went to the next area to pick up the passport and stood in
line until I was called. The official looked at my identification
and picked up an envelope, looked at the picture in the passport,
put it back, and started to shuffle through the envelopes. I said,
"It is mine. My foster daughter is African American." She looked
surprised and embarrassed and apologized profusely. I smiled and
said, "Don't worry about it."

That afternoon, I drove Peter and Martha the three hours to
their grandparents in Albany, while Michael stayed behind to care
for Cecilia and take her to her weekly visit with her birth mother.
I was about to exit the thruway when my cell phone rang. We all
gave a little start. Since I was busy driving, Peter unbuckled his
seatbelt and leaned over from the back seat to fumble in my bag
for the phone. "It's for you," he said.

It was a woman from the foster care agency. With little intro-
duction, she asked me, "Where are the bottles?"

"I'm on the thruway near Albany," I told her.

"The baby is screaming," she said.

Keeping my eye on the road (and envisioning the agency,
which is in the middle of Manhattan surrounded by stores), I
said, "Michael didn't leave any bottles?"

"No."

"Well, he must have fed her beforehand then. She is probably
not hungry, she must be tired."

She then informed me that it is the foster parent's job to bring all the necessary items to the visits. If it hadn't been clear before exactly whose responsibility this child was, it was now.

Three weeks and three days after Cecilia arrived, we set off with her on her first transatlantic adventure. She seemed completely unfazed, spending most of the flight asleep in the little bassinet that hooked to the wall in front of us. Even thousands of miles from home, we couldn't leave our feelings about our new situation behind, and the discussions surrounding them permeated the trip. I looked forward to my sister meeting the baby and to her observations and opinions, which I thought would help me clarify my own feelings. In Hungary, while we still thought and worried about our role, we could also just be two normal parents with an infant. The trip was a welcome respite from the ongoing neighborhood commentary.

Our hotel was located in the Pest side of Budapest, an old city that is at the same time majestic and slightly decrepit. Energized by the beauty around us and the freedom from our normal routines, we spent every waking moment out of our hotel room. Besides eating and walking, we shopped. There were antique stores stuffed with interesting furniture, pictures, and china. There were stores that sold local crafts—beautiful Hungarian embroidery, lace, and pottery. In the back of one toyshop were glass cases with enticing dolls. One was a sweet little brown girl with long black hair who was dressed in a red corduroy skirt and a white sweatshirt. She cost eighty dollars, and I decided to buy her for Cecilia. I recognized the insanity of buying an expensive doll that was more appropriate for a six-year-old than for an eight-week-old baby, but I couldn't help myself. The doll wasn't really for the baby, it was for me. Like an addict who couldn't address her underlying issues, I couldn't control the uncertainties of our mutual situation but I could temporarily play the doting mommy with a quick fix.

I thought about that doll when I later read a book about a woman's experience taking several older children into foster care. One striking thing in the book was the description of the material items the family gave the children. In reference to one child, the author wrote: "We adored her, and we spoiled her. We bought her clothes and dolls and puppets and games and doll cradles; tea sets and dishes, doll clothes and doll suitcases so her dolls would have luggage when we traveled. . . . We felt she had been cheated out of so much of her childhood, and we tried to make up for it with Little Mermaid sheets, and towels with her name and ballerina slippers embroidered on them, a Mickey Mouse alarm clock, and a ballerina watch" (Mansfield 1993, 62).

Perhaps because of their former isolation from the rest of the world, Hungarians are fascinated by black people. I felt as if we were traveling with a royal princess. People would stop, stare, point, and smile. Our Hungarian friend Gabor explained that there are few black people in Hungary and they are therefore thought of as "very cool." After a day in the Jewish quarter with Gabor and his family, with whom we had been communicating in broken English, Gabor's son, age nine, pointed to his mother who was six months pregnant and spoke in Hungarian. His father translated: His son wished that his mother could give birth to such an attractive brown baby.

Gabor was very curious about the U.S. foster care system. I asked him if such a system existed in Hungary. He said that he was unaware of any children in foster care—children without families to care for them lived in orphanages. I asked if those children would have a chance to be adopted, and he answered that many of the children in orphanages were part gypsy and that there was enormous discrimination against gypsies in Hungary. He said that if he were to adopt a gypsy child, he would be concerned about whether the child would be "permitted" to attend college.

On our last day, we crossed the Danube River to the more mountainous Buda side of the city. An old ornate hotel there, the Gellert, had a beautifully tiled interior and a swimming pool whose ceiling opened to the outdoors. To the side of the swimming pool, there was a hot springs area. In this smaller pool, lion heads spout water. We had brought Cecilia's stroller so that we could sit her in it while we went in the hot pool. When Lynn and I emerged from the women's dressing room with the baby, two middle-aged women in white uniforms with white sport socks and white clogs came rushing up to us speaking in Hungarian; I thought they were reproaching us for bringing in the stroller. We looked confused, and one asked, this time in English, "The baby comes from you?"

"No," I said, "she is adopted." (I used this word as I had given up trying to explain foster care.)

"Your husband, he is *brown*?"

"No" I said, "she is from *another* woman's body, a brown woman."

"Oy, *so beautiful*! Wait, wait!" She ran to get a third woman.

"Oh!" They smiled, taking us in, speaking rapidly in Hungarian.

During our visit, Lynn and I began a running commentary that reflected my anxiety about our role in Cecilia's care. We had been talking about the recent media attention in the United States and Europe on Americans' use of video cameras to spy on their babysitters. Lynn jokingly made a little twist on that situation: "Cecilia is probably recording all of this trip on her own little babycam." At that moment, as Cecilia started to wake in her stroller and gave a little cry, Lynn illustrated (using an infant voice): "Violation #36: Ignoring me in my stroller while talking to your sister." Later, in one of the city's many incredible coffee and pastry shops, I was about to indulge in a gigantic piece of tiramisu. I said (using the baby voice): "Violation #57: Eating pastry in front of me when you know perfectly well that I am too young to try any."

Michael and Max, although familiar with Lynn's and my attempts to lessen anxiety with humor, seemed slightly put off by these dramatizations; they chose not to note any "violations" during our vacation.

In our more serious discussions, I told Lynn that while the agency wanted Cecilia to be with one of her half sisters if she couldn't be returned to her mother, I fantasized about her being adopted by a childless black couple. I wanted the best environment for her—adults who would be devoted to her. Lynn asked how I thought that would ever happen. I said that I didn't know but I did know Cecilia was a healthy, lovely baby who was getting excellent care and who I thought would be very desirable to anyone.

April and May went by in a blur. I focused on the day to day. Sometimes I was overwhelmed with Cecilia's sweetness. She ate well and she slept well. She often napped during the afternoon, which gave me some time to make dinner and focus on Peter and Martha and their homework. I would put Peter and Martha to bed at eight o'clock. I used to guard this evening time alone. Now in the late evening Cecilia would wake up, and I coveted time alone with her. I would sit on the couch in the TV room with my feet up and the TV remote, the phone, and a bottle by my side so I wouldn't have to get up. I would arrange Cecilia across my lap with the red-and-white-checked down pillows supporting my arm, which cradled Cecilia's head. I would feed her, smile at her, and let her nap in my arms.

When people asked if it was a shock to have an infant again, I responded, "It is a pleasure." My experiences with my older children all came back to me, and it felt natural, with two exceptions. First, I was not breastfeeding Cecilia and I began to have dreams that I was—dreams that were conflicts between the sweet closeness and my feelings of shame/guilt/embarrassment. In one dream, the caseworkers were shocked and horrified when they found out. I sputtered, "But isn't the breast the best?" while knowing that I had crossed that line between foster parent and parent. Second, I was able to detach from Cecilia at times—with a babysitter for ten hours a week when I went to class and also when I left her with Michael. I wondered about this, as I was inseparable from Peter and Martha the first six months. I decided that a combination of many factors produced the difference. I was ten years older now and had begun a career I loved. Peter and Martha and my nephews were growing into healthy children, so I now knew that mothers needn't be smothering. Also, since I was not breastfeeding, Michael could share more of the baby-care responsibilities. He easily soothed Cecilia, since he was an experienced father and cared for her with confidence. One other factor was that Cecilia came to us at five weeks—she had existed before us and without us. Someone else had attended to her needs. She didn't belong wholly to us.

At times I was almost jubilant at having a lovely little infant without having spent the previous year consumed by pregnancy. I would contemplate all that I had accomplished that wouldn't have been possible if I had been pregnant—this was what it was like to be a father, I thought, having a baby with no effort. The sacrosanctity of breastfeeding was diminished a bit as well, as Cecilia thrived physically and socially.

However, the oddness of the situation was never far away, and sometimes it manifested itself in ways I had never considered. While we thought that Cecilia was a beautiful name, we hadn't chosen it ourselves and it caused a bit of trouble in our household, as our dog was called "Cece." No matter what I said, visitors would naturally refer to the baby as "Cece" and the dog would go crazy, especially when they used the high-pitched baby voice the dog thought was reserved exclusively for her. To alleviate some of

the confusion, Peter and Martha began to call the baby "Kiki."
I used every pet name imaginable, including some I made up
myself.

I continued to take Cecilia to her weekly visits to see her birth
family. The visits took place in various rooms throughout the
agency, some of which were small and stuffy and some of which
were sometimes shared with another family having a visit. Of
course, the agency was in an office building and the spaces where
families met had been designed as offices or meeting rooms. Of
the three rooms that were used, only one had windows. The furniture and the toys were drab, worn, and dirty. Many of the toys
were broken or had missing parts. While families were supposed
to meet and socialize, nothing about the environment suggested
a home. I found the space impersonal and depressing. I complained about the toys and the dirty food crumbs on several occasions. The caseworkers were sympathetic and said that they just
couldn't keep up with the wear and tear from so many families. I
felt bad for them and also recognized that this was not necessarily
the caseworkers' responsibility. On the other hand, I found it in-
excusable; the agency and the caseworkers were supposed to be
modeling appropriate behavior for these families. If necessary, the
rooms and toys should have been scrubbed between visits so that
the space was clean, orderly, and respectful.

Perhaps influenced by the space, the visits seemed chaotic.
While I didn't stay for the visits, I would often pop in at the end
to say hello or to take some pictures. I felt hesitant to impose myself on their private time to take the photos, but no one seemed
to mind and I thought it was important that someone record their
get-togethers. Most of the visits included the birth mother, her
mother, and the five girls. Two of the girls would become very
wound up during the visits, running and jumping and adding to
the chaos. When I suggested that the staff could help structure

the visit time to make it more pleasant, the social worker said that birth parents were evaluated on how well they performed during the visits with their children. The social workers were just there to monitor (and record). I wondered how well I would do, seeing my children once a week in one of those rooms.

The visits epitomized the confusion surrounding the foster care relationships. Sometimes it seemed that the birth mother's and my needs were in direct conflict. The visits seemed too frequent to me in terms of how they disrupted my Wednesday afternoons. But they also seemed too infrequent to keep Cecilia bonded to her mother. With the exception of the two hours on Wednesday nights and a few hours of babysitting, Michael and I were the only caretakers of this child. Some weeks after Cecilia came to live with us, I noticed that she was upset when I picked her up from the visits. I could hear her crying as the family approached the waiting room. A few times I overhead staff refer to her as "colicky." "She is not colicky," I would say quietly. "I don't think I have ever met a more easygoing baby. She is a dream." Cecilia would quiet as soon as I took her in my arms. This was disturbing to me and embarrassing at the same time—like being the center of attention on someone else's birthday.

On Wednesdays, in the few minutes Cecilia's mother and I spent together, I was supposed to model appropriate parenting behavior for her. I felt that she couldn't care less what I did as long as she got to see her children. I was interested in getting to know the family better because they were part of Cecilia, but otherwise I had no bond or relationship with them. They had no reason to have an interest in me, and while I tried to act as polite and as considerate as I could, my actions were motivated in part by guilt, and that was a difficult way to begin a relationship.

Each week I shared tidbits about Cecilia's development. When I took pictures, I always got a second set. I would sort the pictures of Cecilia—one set for her baby book and the others carefully divided between her mother and our own family photo albums. However much I tried, my ability to share the parenting wore thin at times, sometimes at a primal level: After the visits, I started feeling compelled to change Cecilia's clothing. It reminded me of when Peter and Martha were little and came home from the babysitter smelling of her house—it always bothered me. With Cecilia, it wasn't a good smell/bad smell thing (the birth mom was often better groomed than I was). It was a deeper attachment: You, the baby, are an extension of me—a psychological kind of thing. Whenever I thought about this, it reminded me of an article I once read about animals imprinting their scent on their young as part of the bonding process.

Sometimes I stayed in the waiting room during the visits, trying to intercept the other girls' caretakers to gather information. It took me many months to figure out who all the players were in this complex family. We were never formally introduced, and initially I felt quite timid around them, wondering what they thought of me and feeling out what an appropriate relationship should be. I did want to get to know the others, and I was interested in working together as a team; however, I sensed that they were more interested in maintaining their independence, perhaps wary of trusting each other, the caseworkers, and the birth family. Sierra's grandfather was quite friendly, but he blamed Zuri, the birth mother, for interfering with his and his son's relationship with Sierra and therefore didn't like Zuri very much. He also seemed overwhelmed with his other family responsibilities. Simone, the foster mother of Brittney and MaryKate, was an immigrant from Jamaica and a Jehovah's Witness. She and her husband, a mechanic, had a birth son a few years younger than MaryKate. Simone was a stay-at-home mother and was motivated to take in children from foster care because of her religious beliefs and her husband's enthusiasm. She took a tough-love approach, often complaining how difficult the girls were but then telling me how she got up at 5:00 AM to iron their dresses for school and fix their hair. Simone became my most reliable source of information, as she was the person I saw most frequently and was the most talkative. Dawn lived with Lorraine, who had taken her in at birth. Dawn seemed quite attached to Lorraine, but Lorraine was a bit elusive and often was late for or missed visits.

Michael and I were both unnerved and intimidated at times during the visits. Michael shared a story with me that was both hilarious and pathetic. During one of the first visits he attended, it was quite cold and he had brought Cecilia on the train in the Snugli. After the visit, Cecilia was handed to him and he started to get her ready to go. One of Cecilia's birth aunts who had attended the visit said to Michael in a way that felt critical to him, "It is cold outside. Where is her snowsuit?" Michael had brought along an L.L. Bean "baby bag" that a good friend had given us for Peter and that looks a little different from a traditional snowsuit. He tried to explain that the baby bag was very warm but felt increasingly flustered as he stood there, beginning to sweat, everyone staring at him, unable to get Cecilia's legs into the appropriate holes of the Snugli.

Although I never had a cross word with Cecilia's birth family, there always seems to be an underlying tension implicit in the relationship between parents and foster parents. This tension was evident during one weekly visit in my interactions with another birth parent. I stepped off the elevator and as usual signed in at the receptionist's desk—my name in the column labeled "client/ visitor" (I was unsure which of these categories I fell under), the name of the person I was going to see, the department (in this column people stated the reason for their visit), and the time I arrived. I sat in one of the gray fabric chairs in the waiting room with Cecilia on my lap. As usual, the waiting room was chaotic, with children of all ages running around. Next to me on this particular day was a black woman—"Birth mother or foster mother?"

I always played this little guessing game with myself—with two young girls, about two and four years old, dressed in purple and blue matching nylon running suits with bandanas on their heads. The younger girl was eating chocolate and, naturally, dripping some on herself. The mess seemed to be causing the woman great stress. After the child finished her treat, the woman carefully wiped the child's face, her hands, and the front of her suit while the child squirmed. The woman then took the bandana off each child. After that she carefully removed the swim caps underneath that held their neatly coiffed hair in place.

Comments from passing agency staff confirmed what I had guessed from watching her excruciating attention to their appearance: One of the girls had just been returned to her birth mother that week, and the mother was bringing them to check in with the social worker. I asked the mother how old the girls were. She asked me Cecilia's age and whose child she was. I said that I was the foster mother. The woman then looked me right in the eye and said, "It is going to be awfully hard to give her back to her real mother."

The moment was excruciating. While I appreciated her solidarity with and support of a birth parent she had never met, her comment clarified the distance between us. She either didn't want or didn't trust my support. I wanted to say, I am not preying on your children, don't worry. I could only imagine what she was struggling with, trying to keep her life together while resuming (or maybe for the first time?) taking care of her children.

At this point, Michael and I were doing exactly what we had set out to do. We were nurturing this baby, protecting her, until she returned to her mother or a permanent home could be found for her. It wasn't easy for any of us, this in-between kind of love. I would tell Martha and Peter to think of it as babysitting; we were loving her while we had her but we were a *foster* family. Every time someone asked about her, Martha would stand in front of me on her tiptoes, her uplifted face stretched in a fake smile, and say in a squeaky voice, "Can we adopt her?" People thought it was cute, but I found it disturbing because I could sense Martha's anxiety. I finally pulled her aside and we talked about the situation and she stopped.

Peter said to me one night, "Mommy, I know you said we should think of it like babysitting, but it is hard. It doesn't seem like we are babysitting." He was right. Babysitting has a finite beginning and end. I took the kids to visits occasionally so that they could see Cecilia's birth family, to help them understand that she had a family that cared about her.

I found it hard too. After the initial excitement wore off, I began to think about what I had done. I was finishing up my last class at school, and the rest of my time was devoted to Cecilia. I could have hired a babysitter beyond the ten hours I needed for my class, but I couldn't bring myself to do so. I was a "career mother" of sorts; I had set ways of doing things and I couldn't relinquish what felt like my responsibilities to someone besides Michael. I reviewed my expectations going into foster parenting—I expected to provide a home to a visiting baby, we would all do our own thing, and our schedules would overlap at times. But this was impossible. I knew from my experience with Peter and Martha that parenting was an enormous commitment of time and energy, but somehow I deluded myself into thinking it would require less commitment. I was just finishing my master's in social work, a big accomplishment for me after years of staying at home with the kids. I was scared of being sucked back into a world where I didn't have any professional direction. I started feeling angry that state and national governments expect parents to take care of other people's children without paying them a salary, only a small stipend to cover some of the children's expenses. I worried about other foster parents who had taken in many children. How could they sustain the energy to bond with these children again and again? I wondered if it was necessary for a child's healthy development to have an intense bond. I wondered how attached is attached enough. And I wondered if a parent could be kind and caring but not attached and if this would be enough. I thought about why foster parenting was different from parenting Peter and Martha: They were work but they were also my prizes, because their well-developing selves were my reward for my investment. With Cecilia, I would put in that work and someone else would reap the reward. I questioned whether I was selfless enough to do this.

I began reading a book called *Mother Nature: A History of Mothers, Infants, and Natural Selection*. The author, Sarah Blaffer Hrdy, is an anthropologist, and she approaches the subject of motherhood with extensive knowledge of research on animals. Hrdy provides a framework in which to think of human motherhood. She makes a very convincing case that mothers are "multifaceted strategists" on behalf of their offspring, not just unlimited fountains of love. Consciously or unconsciously, I read this book looking for some way to put my role as a foster parent in context. Hrdy writes of human mothers' need to have helpers to raise their offspring. She also talks about the difficulty of finding substitute caregivers for children due to the complexities of the attachment that develops between mothers and their children. Her mock ad for a modern caregiver could be an ad for a foster parent, except that in place of "low pay" it would state "no pay":

> WANTED: Someone to turn his/her life over to the whims and needs of a smaller, weaker, often unreasonable individual for a period of months or years. Low pay. Little prestige. No security or long-term obligations; faint prospect that any relationship formed will be maintained over time. (Hrdy 1999, 504)

Early in the book Hrdy talks about how researchers have gotten virgin mice, when exposed to newborn pups from another mother mouse, to start lactating and care for them. Hrdy says that the neural pathways change in mice who care for newborns at critical early stages. I felt that, as a mother who has given birth to and cared for two infants, my brain and my body began to react automatically when given an infant to whom I have no familial ties, even if my emotions were in conflict as I tried to walk the tightrope of attachment. My dreams about breastfeeding were an example of my body's automatic pilot.

Several months after Cecilia's arrival, I still found it difficult to answer questions about my attachment—my feelings were private, but some people's curiosity caused them to constantly probe, probably a result of their unfamiliarity and discomfort. I tried to point out that foster parenting wasn't about doing something for yourself, it was about doing something for someone else. I began to feel solidarity with people I knew who had adopted children. These parents seem to understand the necessity of a third party as a caretaker between birth family and adoptive family. They had experience with foster parents or orphanage caretakers. They understood and appreciated the incredible value in this role. I thought back to a visit to some friends, Joe and Claire, who live in Pittsburgh and have an adopted son from Korea. In their kitchen, I had picked up a picture of a Korean woman with a baby strapped to her in a pouch. I asked if it was their son's birth mother. "No," Claire said, "it is his foster mother. She was very attached to our son and we keep in touch with letters." When I talked to people who adopted, it gave me strength and courage to go on in this role—to be the temporary caretaker.

By June, I had stopped obsessing so much and life began to feel more normal. Most people we knew had met Cecilia, and questions about her became less frequent. One day in the middle of the month, during a routine conversation with the social worker,

I was somewhat distracted, looking out the window with pride at our growing garden, when it struck me that it was June—the month that I had been told Cecilia would be moved. My stomach flipped and my hands felt shaky. I interrupted the social worker. "I just realized it's June. What is the plan for Cecilia's move?" To my relief, she responded that the other foster mother wasn't ready to take Cecilia because the little boy there still hadn't moved back with his birth mother. The social worker was quite vague as to when exactly this would happen. Although my nature is to press for details and action, at that moment, I preferred uncertainty to change.

3

Help, American-Style

WHEN MICHAEL and I became foster parents, we learned how stigmatizing, demoralizing, and just plain inconvenient and time consuming being part of the "unentitled" population can be. With the exception of Early Intervention, we often felt that the programs were more concerned with regulating our behavior than with providing services. As a foster parent, I took on a role; when I accepted services and a stipend for the benefit of my foster daughter, I was no longer a middle-class citizen. Although sometimes my experiences made me feel like quitting foster parenthood, I tried to focus on what foster parenting really should be about—the day-to-day caring for Cecilia. I felt deep gratitude that, independent of my foster parent role, my family and I did not have to rely on any of the available social services.

One of the first courses I took to get my master's in social work was in social policy. I hadn't been looking forward to this class, thinking that it would be dry material, mostly names and dates. To my surprise, I found it fascinating. I had never thought about the social programs offered in the United States from an academic perspective. As a consumer and a mother of young children, I had used medical systems in three countries and could see big differences in price, convenience, and support, but it was only later that I understood that these reflected social policy choices. My policy class made me think about the social programs we have in the United States. I was especially fascinated by the basic idea that choices or assumptions underlie all government decisions to fund some programs over others. On September 18, 1996, as Professor Staller lectured, I wrote in my notebook: "Social welfare policy is the response to a social problem or need resulting in the identification and/or collection of resources, and the allocation and redistribution of those resources to alleviate the problems or the well-being of individuals or groups." Or, as I had written more simply in my first class the week before: "Policy is about an 'in group' and an 'out group.'"

There are tremendous numbers of groups in need of resources in the United States, and many factors are taken into consideration when prioritizing their perceived needs. When a society decides how much money a group is going to get, one factor that influences its choices is whether enough people consider the group deserving. Poor people, not known to be educated and well-connected advocates for themselves, are not always considered deserving; they are often thought of as "lazy" or as responsible for their own condition. Journalist Nina Bernstein writes on the New York City foster care system in *The Lost Children of Wilder: The Epic Struggle to Change Foster Care*: "There has long been an iron rule in American social welfare policy: conditions must be worse for the dependent poor than for anyone who works." She follows with a statement I did not fully understand until I became a foster parent: "The seldom-acknowledged corollary is that the subsidized care of other people's children must be undesirable enough, or scarce enough, to play a role in this system of deterrence"—which basically means that foster care has got to be bad enough that you wouldn't be tempted to willingly put your own children in that system (Bernstein 2001a, 13).

Groups who might need resources are pretty easy to identify— old, handicapped, young, sick, or poor people. What isn't easy is figuring out a system that allocates limited resources fairly. Three factors can affect how much money different groups get for services to help them: first, whether the group is considered deserving; second, whether the group's condition is universal (we will all be old one day, but we will not all have a chronic disease); third, whether society feels it has something to gain from improving the condition of the group (vaccination programs and educated people benefit everyone).

These same factors can also affect how the services or money are delivered to individuals. For example, if two people receive monthly stipends for two hundred dollars from the government, but the checks are funded by different programs, why does one person get a check in the mail while the other person has to go to a certain office (which isn't necessarily in that person's neighborhood) at 10:00 AM on the third Wednesday of the month and stand in line to receive a check? I thought that as a foster parent I would be part of the solution to a problem, not the person standing in line on the third Wednesday of the month. In fact, it became overwhelmingly obvious that I was merely a cog in a large system designed to serve children of the poor.

As a social worker, I was familiar with all four of the programs that I would use as a foster parent: Medicaid (a federally and state-financed program that provides health coverage primarily for low-income women and children); WIC (an acronym for the Special

Supplemental Food Program for Women, Infants, and Children—a federal nutrition program for low-income pregnant or breastfeeding women and children up to age five); Early Intervention (physical and developmental therapies for children under the age of three); and the larger foster care system itself. I knew that all four programs were funded through a combination of federal and state dollars. However, I was completely naïve about how it felt to actually use them. Of these programs, two (WIC and Medicaid) were based on financial need. Early Intervention was universal in that it was available to those at any income level, as long as it was determined that the child needed the services. And the foster care system, in theory, would serve any children whose parents abused or neglected them, but in fact almost exclusively serves the poorest, least educated people in America. Significantly, the federal funding which pays for a considerable portion of foster care expenses is an entitlement program only for children whose families meet the poverty guidelines under Title IV-E of the Social Security Act. My experiences with each program, including how easy the program was to use and how I was treated, reflected the assumptions of the middle-class managers who set up the programs for poor people.

Medicaid

On March 14, when Cecilia was seven weeks old, I took her to see my own children's pediatrician, Dr. Goodwin. Initially I was told that I was obligated to take Cecilia to the foster care agency for all well-baby checkups. But when Cecilia was sick, I was permitted to take her to a doctor in our neighborhood or to the emergency room. I wanted to make sure Dr. Goodwin was familiar with the baby, since she would provide the sick-baby care. Dr. Goodwin was doing this as a favor to me, as most pediatricians provide all the care for children, not care just for ill children. I also wanted to make sure that Cecilia had a complete checkup by someone I trusted. Dr. Goodwin concurred with my opinion that the baby seemed healthy and developmentally appropriate, but she advised me that in the case of family risk factors or an incomplete medical history, it was better to have an evaluation by an Early Intervention program. As she concluded the exam, Dr. Goodwin said to me, "As my father would have said"—and here she assumed a British accent—"this baby has landed with her butt in the butta." I was flattered. I felt that the pediatrician who had known me for several years was saying that I could add something of value to this child's life because of my skills as a parent.

When she asked about how our foster parent experience was going so far, I mentioned our difficulty getting a prescription for eyedrops for Cecilia. As a child in foster care, Cecilia had a Medicaid card that was supposed to pay for prescriptions and medical care. However, as we discovered, almost none of the pharmacies in our neighborhood accepted Medicaid. The one exception was a large chain pharmacy that I generally avoided because it was so disorganized. When I went there to get the prescription filled, the situation was compounded by the pharmacy's interaction with the Medicaid people. I was given a prescription for eyedrops for Cecilia because she appeared to have an infection in one of her eyes. The pharmacist told me that she couldn't fill the prescription because the computers weren't working in the Medicaid office for several days. It concerned me to have to wait, but as new members to the foster care system, we were not thinking for ourselves and acting independently, we were following the rules as we had been instructed to do. Days passed, and we started to worry that the little infection was going to permanently harm Cecilia's eye. After a week of trying to get the prescription through Medicaid, we gave up and paid twenty-five dollars for the prescription. Dr. Goodwin was as disgusted as I was by this pathetic system and urged me to try and get other neighborhood pharmacies to sign up for Medicaid so that I could use them instead.

The only problem with using Dr. Goodwin was that on average

she charged a hundred dollars per visit and Medicaid only paid about fifty dollars per visit. Michael and I talked it over and decided that it was well worth the convenience and the confidence we had in the pediatric practice to pay the difference. We were impressed already with our doctor's recommendation to have an Early Intervention evaluation. Michael later found out that, to our amazement, our private health insurance would cover Cecilia. And so for a while, we were pleased with the system—well-baby visits at the agency, sick care and periodic checkups at our neighborhood pediatric practice with our private health insurance covering the extra expenses.

Only much later did our satisfactory system come to a halt. When I made an offhand comment about our private insurance to the nurse at the agency one day over the telephone, she asked me to hold on, and the nursing supervisor got on the telephone and told me that using our private medical insurance was absolutely prohibited. The agency was getting paid for medical care for Cecilia, and therefore we needed to use the Medicaid that was arranged through them or else they would be getting paid for something that they weren't providing, and they could get in big trouble for Medicaid fraud. Using our private doctor was not allowed either; we were supposed to be using Cecilia's Medicaid card at hospital clinics (where no doubt we would have long waits and a different doctor for each visit). I had experience with these clinics as a social work intern: My client would be given a nine o'clock appointment along with twenty other people, and patients would be taken in the order in which they signed in at the front desk. Often there weren't even enough chairs for everyone.

The agency never offered to stop accepting payment for Cecilia's medical care so that I could provide higher-quality, more convenient medical care through our private insurance. Nor did they offer an explanation as to why they couldn't do so. Sometimes I felt like an anonymous number as a foster parent. Because there are so many children in foster care from troubled families, it seemed that the only way to ensure basic care was to adhere to a rigid checklist. No allowances or bonuses were offered for building a reputation as a responsible and reliable caregiver that might allow foster parents to skirt a particular rule in a way that wouldn't hurt the child in their care.

My experience with this system was such a contrast to the interactions I had with the medical systems in Europe. When we lived in the Netherlands, Peter was an infant (from seven weeks to thirteen months old), and when we lived in Belgium, Martha was an infant and toddler (from six months to three years old). When they were sick, I didn't take them to a private pediatrician unless something was seriously wrong. I took them to a general practitioner who treated the whole family. If the children were too sick to get to the doctor or if it was after hours, a doctor would come to the house. For checkups and immunizations, I took Peter and Martha to well-baby clinics in the neighborhoods where we lived. Even though we weren't citizens of those countries, the children were entitled to free immunizations and checkups. Around these clinics, other supports were built in. Appointments were given to children of the same age at the same time, so mothers in similar situations got to meet each other. In The Hague, the social worker who was part of the team came to our apartment to see where Peter was sleeping (to make sure the mattress and crib were safe, etc.), and when he started to crawl, she offered to come again to help baby proof.

Early Intervention

Following our pediatrician's recommendation, I called some Early Intervention programs and found one called Significant Steps that specialized in evaluating very young babies. Early Intervention programs are federally and state-funded programs that evaluate children under the age of three to see if they need services such as physical or occupational therapy or special education. The overall program is extraordinary in that the services are provided in the child's home, free of charge, regardless of income. Three women from my neighborhood with professional qualifications in the early intervention field had started Significant Steps approximately eight years earlier. I was entitled to pick any agency that suited our needs, and I chose their program because they seemed knowledgeable and friendly and they were within walking distance from our house.

For our initial visit, Monday morning, April 10, a social worker came to my house with another woman from Significant Steps. They were both black, and I worried that they would disapprove of a white woman caring for a black baby. The social worker, Evita, and her co-worker admired the house as I led them into the kitchen. I felt slightly embarrassed by the attention. They asked to hold Cecilia. "Isn't she sweet—what a little doll!" they exclaimed. Evita asked me about her birth history, our family composition, and my reasons for requesting a referral, her questions interspersed with cooing and cuddling of the baby. They admired the baby and referred to me as "Mommy." I loved it. I welcomed the confidence with which they clarified my relationship to Cecilia and eased my fears as to whether I was an appropriate caretaker.

When Cecilia became fussy, Evita instructed her co-worker to return her to me. I had realized sometimes when someone else held her that although we thought of Cecilia as a very easygoing baby, we had also learned what made her happy. She rarely cried, but we never let her cry long. Now I placed her in the crook of my arm, gave her the pacifier, and softly rocked her. She relaxed and fell asleep immediately. "Oh, look at her," Evita said. "She loves her mommy." The co-worker, slightly miffed that she didn't have the touch, mumbled, "I didn't know she took a pacifier."

The Thursday morning following the initial interview, a team of four came to do the evaluation. The women marched in single file through our narrow entrance hall. They introduced themselves in the living room where we had more room to spread out—the occupational therapist, the physical therapist, the early education specialist, and Evita, the social worker. We moved the coffee table to make space for everyone in the living room and laid Cecilia in the center on a blanket on the rug. I watched in amazement as the specialists looked at Cecilia's reflexes and responses. They explained her every movement and why it was significant in terms of her ongoing motor development. They also rang a little bell on each side of her head, checking her hearing. When they finished the evaluation, they packed up to go, telling me that they would call soon to arrange a meeting to discuss the results. I was left with a feeling of respect and gratitude toward these women and their program due to their professionalism, their knowledge, and their consideration; I knew that I could trust them. I really felt supported by this Early Intervention program.

Part of my interest in and enthusiasm for Early Intervention services was the result of our experience with Peter. Peter was a perfectly healthy and intelligent baby, although he had difficulty learning to talk. While the pediatrician was concerned by the time of Peter's second birthday, I was impressed with the hand signals our son had invented to indicate his wishes. For example, he would hold his hands together to show that he wanted his mittens. By the age of three, Peter stared at my mouth while I was talking and people commented that his speech was unintelligible. When I had his hearing tested, the audiologist said that he could hear fine. The problem was a mystery until kindergarten, when he was unable to learn the alphabet or numbers. A learning specialist discovered that although Peter could hear, he had auditory processing problems that caused sounds to be unclear. She said that he had a language-based learning disability. It was only then that we made a connection between Peter's difficulties and the history of dyslexia in Michael's family. The next few years were filled with intensive one-on-one tutoring. I spent hours every week coordinating Peter's services and helping him. When at the end of second grade, after much hard work and help from a brilliant tutor, Peter made a breakthrough and began reading books of his choosing, Michael and I were jubilant.

The relationships we developed with the people who helped Peter and the progress he made inspired me to see the potential in all children. It also made me an avid supporter of extra services and very disturbed when I saw children or adults who had missed out on services that could have improved their lives. I thought about Cecilia's mother. I knew that she was mildly retarded, and I had learned with a bit of research that this meant she should have been able to achieve skills of up to about a sixth-grade level (American Psychological Association 1994). From what I could gather, she didn't seem to have reached this level, and I wondered what her childhood had been like. I knew also from my research that mental retardation is rarely inherited, although it can be in conditions like Down syndrome. Its etiology is often not clear, but it can result from problems in pregnancy, illnesses in infancy, or severe social or environmental deprivation, among other things. In Sweden, where there are superior social services and few poor people, the rate of mild (but not severe) retardation is many times less than the rate in the United States (Sameroff 1986). While Cecilia did not seem delayed to me, she did qualify for Early Intervention services, in part because of her uncertain history. I willingly accepted them. She loved the extra attention and I intended to give her every advantage that her mother's family appeared to have been denied.

About the same time as the Early Intervention evaluation, I had our first home visit from the foster care agency. The two offered an interesting contrast. At the agency, you are assigned to a team that consists of a social worker, a supervisor, a case assistant, and a nurse from the Medical Department (the doctors vary). The social workers are busy with paperwork at the agency and with court appearances, so the home visits are most often conducted by the case assistants. While this is perfectly understandable from a workload perspective, it is also a shame. The social workers who make many important decisions regarding the child never get to see the child at home, where she would be most relaxed. In addition, there is such a high turnover of case assistants and social workers at foster care agencies that consistent observations over time are impossible. Quality foster care really requires individual assessments, and foster parents need the support.

The foster care support is so different from the Early Intervention program, which is almost exclusively home based and where, over time, the parent and the physical therapist, teacher, or speech therapist build a relationship. Joint decisions can be made regarding the child because the Early Intervention provider really knows the child and because there is mutual trust between the parent and the provider. Another difference in the way relationships develop between parents and Early Intervention program staff compared to foster parents and agency staff is that there seems to be so much more clarity regarding the work in Early Intervention—the programs are helping children develop, they aren't making complex decisions with multiple party involvement.

The foster care caseworker, Ronald, was polite and pleasant but he didn't come to offer me help. He came to look at Cecilia and make sure she seemed well and safe. He came to make sure I had diapers, formula, clothing, a place for Cecilia to sleep, smoke detectors, and window guards. And Ronald was obligated not just to ask me if I had provided these things for the baby but to see them all for himself. So I led him through the house, opening cupboards, pressing the buttons on the smoke detectors to make sure the batteries were fresh, and pointing out window guards.

Ronald, like all agency employees, began the visit by calling me

Mrs. Gerstenzang (or some variation of Gerstenzang, as this name is always difficult for people). I assured him that he should just call me Sarah. I did this because my first name is easier to pronounce and remember and because everyone I know calls me by my first name. Agency employees introduce themselves by their first and last names and are called by their first names (except for the doctors, of course). Although there may be cultural reasons that other foster parents prefer to be referred to in a more formal way, to me the formality felt false, like a mockery at times, since there were few other demonstrations of respect. I had a working relationship with these people; I talked to someone at the agency almost every week; and yet no one called me by my first name, even when I asked them to do so repeatedly.

During this visit, I tried to get more information about Cecilia's birth family, as Ronald made visits to Cecilia's half siblings' foster homes as well as to us. I asked him if he had visited the other girls in their homes. He said he had. I wondered if some type of confidentiality prevented him from sharing details with me about Cecilia's half sisters. I also asked if he knew anything about Cecilia's mother and her situation. He said he thought she might have been in foster care growing up. I was stunned by this (possible) revelation. I wanted to know more, but that was all Ronald offered. He remarked that after years of work in social services, while he intellectually realized that it was not true, he sometimes felt that there was a genetic marker for foster care. I looked at him questioningly, and he explained that in a notable number of his cases where the children are in foster care, the children's parents or grandparents had also been in foster care. In other words, whatever led to the placement of the child's relatives, the foster care system didn't seem to offer a better alternative for them: History was repeating itself.

At the end of April, we traveled to Washington, D.C., for the weekend, as Michael had to attend a partners' meeting there. Anytime we left New York State, I needed to ask the agency's permission, and the agency in turn had to get signed consent from the mother. This wasn't always so simple, because although I had the direct telephone number of Cecilia's social worker at the agency, she was understandably not always at her desk. Each time she didn't pick up her phone right away, my heart sank, because it would be the beginning of a long line of transfers around the agency until I left a message with some anonymous person. Modern phone systems did not exist at our agency and therefore voice mail was not an option.

To meet the travel rules, I also had to give the social worker the name, address, and telephone number of the hotel where we would be staying, as well as the name and telephone number of the nearest hospital. While it seemed reasonable for them to know where we were going, I couldn't think of one reason why the social worker's having the name and number of the nearest hospital would keep Cecilia any safer.

While in Washington, D.C., I took the kids around Georgetown and to the Mall to see the monuments, but I also wanted to meet up with some old friends. In anticipation of this, I had called the hotel from New York before we left to hire a babysitter for one evening. I didn't like leaving the kids with someone I didn't know, but it was a welcome break for me, and I rationalized it by saying that at least the older kids always seemed thrilled to have a new adult care for them. When I called this time, I asked the concierge if the hotel's babysitters were over twenty-one and had child-abuse background checks. He assured me that they did. Not wanting to sound paranoid and because I doubted whether child-abuse background checks really make kids safer, I felt obliged to say *I* wasn't worried but that as foster parents, we were required by the agency to ask. I am sure my long-winded explanation only confirmed for the concierge that I was insane.

In any event, hiring this babysitter, who turned out to be a very nice, mature woman reminiscent of Mary Poppins, caused me much angst. I made sure there was plenty of time to explain all that Cecilia needed and when I left the room, I spent some time in the hallway with my ear pressed to the door to make sure no one was screaming. My anxiety came from the usual worries any parents have when leaving their child with someone they don't know. And it came from the knowledge that the omnipotent foster care agency could remove Cecilia from our home at anytime.

After you have been a foster parent to a child in your home for a year, in New York State you are entitled to a hearing if a child is removed from your home against your wishes and sent anywhere except back to the birth family. However, before that time, you are at the mercy of an agency that doesn't create most of the regulations but must enforce them. Complicating this are unreasonable and excessive rules that the agency may not enforce but can use as evidence of noncompliance if it chooses to.

When I returned to the hotel room, Martha proudly informed me that they had given Cecilia a bath. I was momentarily alarmed, imagining all the potential hazards. I could envision the *Washington Post* headline: "Foster Child Removed from Lawyer's Family's Care, Injured in Bathtub When Left with Unauthorized Babysitter." Despite my worries, the children were all fine, cheerful, and apparently well cared for.

On the train ride home, with lots of songs, cooing, and silly exaggerated facial expressions, I got Cecilia to smile for the first time, and therefore won an ongoing contest with Michael. We had been giving it our all for more than a week—trying to get that first sweet smile.

The sense of vulnerability continued to haunt us. One weekend we traveled to upstate New York to attend Michael's aunt's wedding. I didn't need to get the agency's permission because we were still in New York State. When we left on our two-day trip,

Cecilia had a cold and it seemed to get worse by the hour. She fell asleep in my arms during the wedding ceremony, only rousing briefly due to her hacking cough. In the row ahead of us, people kept turning around to look at us. At the reception, her nose was oozing green mucus and Michael's father, who is a doctor, insisted that she needed a prescription for antibiotics. It seemed that much of the rest of the reception was focused on Cecilia, her illness, and what medication should be used to treat her. I was used to the ongoing medical discussions at Michael's family gatherings by now. Michael's grandparents had owned a pharmacy, and every get-together seemed to focus on some ailment; it was part of their unique family culture. Michael's aunt and her husband, both pharmacists, opened their pharmacy to fill the prescription after their wedding reception ended.

We gave Cecilia the first dose of the medications before we put her to bed at the hotel. But around 1:00 AM, I woke up because her breathing from the portacrib next to our bed sounded so irregular. I lifted her from the crib and could feel the heat emanating from her body. I woke Michael in a panic and we sat in bed trying to decide what we should do. Cecilia lay limp in her pink fleece sleeper, draped across my legs. I gave her some infant ibuprofen to bring down her fever, but we felt overwhelmed with worry. Should we take her to the hospital just to be safe? We were required to call the agency first and let them know if we decided to do that. The question in the back of my mind was, What would the agency say if they knew she was out of New York City and that relatives had diagnosed her and filled a prescription for her? In the end, we decided to wait and monitor her fever. By the next day, she began to recover.

While I don't think fear of the agency's disapproval was a factor in our decision not to take Cecilia to the hospital that night, I wondered how many times foster parents hesitated to seek help because they felt they would be judged harshly or inappropriately.

The question always lurked there for me: What would the agency say? I considered myself a responsible parent, but having a foster care agency (and the Administration for Children's Services) as your co-parent with the real authority could be unnerving. Unlike a "marriage" with love and trust between the parents, we always had the sense that the agency was looking over our shoulder and evaluating our actions, whether it was qualified to do so or not.

An agency social worker once reluctantly admitted to me that she preferred foster parents who had nothing else going on in their lives (such as a job), because they could comply with all the time-consuming regulations. The social worker, who had to work within the confines of the agency schedule, was focused on how difficult it was to find a time when foster parents could bring the children to meet with their birth parents. Since the agency wasn't open on the weekend, it had to be during the week. It didn't matter whether the time was inconvenient to the foster parents, as long as they attended the required weekly visits and it was documented in the case file.

In our situation, because some of Cecilia's half siblings went to school, the visits had to be in the late afternoon during the week. Having thoughtlessly chosen an agency in another borough, that meant I had to bring Cecilia an hour on the subway in each direction at dinner time, packing something for the two of us to eat. Naturally, she was tired and fussy at this time. Because of the significant flights of stairs on both ends of the trip, at first I took Cecilia in the Snugli. When she got too big for that (which wasn't long, as she quickly moved to the ninety-sixth percentile for height and weight), I switched to a backpack. When I could no longer support her weight in the backpack during the walking part of the trip, I took the stroller and the backpack, putting her into the backpack while I was on the stairs because carrying her in the stroller on the stairs hurt my neck. Eventually, I had to use a car service that cost twenty-five dollars each way. When I explained my difficulty to the agency and asked that they share the cost, the social worker apologetically said that they only reimbursed foster parents for carfare if the foster parent had to travel with three children under the age of five.

I also had to hire a babysitter for my other two children for the four hours the trip took. I couldn't help Peter and Martha with their homework until I got home, and they were unhappy that I was gone each Wednesday afternoon and evening. I often felt guilty because it seemed unfair to them. I considered refusing to go to the visits and telling the agency to have one of their employees pick Cecilia up and return her, but I never dared. You can be the best foster parent in the world, but you learn quickly that you must follow the rules. I was upset when I heard about another infant being removed after two months from a great foster home with two working parents; with their work schedules, they could manage only a Friday-morning visit, and the school-aged siblings, who were in another foster home, had to come in the afternoon. While I understood the importance of family visits, the flip side of some of these regulations was that potentially excellent foster parents might be excluded because they couldn't tailor their lives to the agency schedule.

My thesaurus has the following synonyms for the word "foster": back, champion, support, uphold, entertain, harbor, house, lodge, shelter, accommodate, assist, favor, help, oblige. We were prepared to do all those things as foster parents. What we weren't interested in doing was going to useless training, having to get permission to go on vacation, getting reprimanding letters in the mail when we were behind on some regulation (regardless of whether we were at fault), and spending time on paperwork that had to do with agency business, not with parenting. But we did all those things. And we had a good agency, as foster care agencies go, rated number three out of about forty agencies in New York City with a score that placed it in the "excellent" category. One of the most straightforward supportive things the agency did for us was to provide a carseat and crib when Cecilia outgrew the infant carseat and bassinet my friend had lent us. I mentioned our need to the social worker, and within a few days the items were delivered to our door. And we were fortunate that the social workers we dealt with all seemed reasonable and intelligent, although some were inexperienced. But the agency is a business; it has a contract with the city and must comply with federal and state laws that guide agency policies and practices.

WIC

On Wednesday, May 24, I took Cecilia in for her four-month checkup at the agency's third-floor office and wondered what the other tenants thought about the number of children going in and out of the elevators. In the agency space, there were some great black-and-white photographs on the walls showing the children the agency has worked with over the decades. Early photos show white children, whereas those taken in more recent years have predominately black children; less than 5 percent of the children now in foster care in New York City are white. The old photos reflect a time when private agencies (which received public funds) that were primarily Catholic and Jewish in New York City were able to select the children they served based on their religious affiliation.

The checkup went well. When the nurse made an offhand comment about how healthy Cecilia was, I felt greedy for details and pressed her to clarify what she meant. I asked what kind of problems the other children she sees might have. She said, "All kinds," and vaguely referred to emotional and developmental problems. I wondered what combination of genetics and environment was responsible for Cecilia's remarkable development. The doctor too commented on Cecilia's health, especially her exceptional social responsiveness.

Afterward, I took the subway to downtown Brooklyn for our appointment at the WIC office. The agency had told me that our foster daughter was eligible for free formula and cereal through the WIC program. This was my second appointment with WIC, where I had to go every two months to pick up vouchers that I could exchange at my local grocery store. I was half an hour early for my one o'clock appointment (naively, I hoped this might cut down on the wait I had experienced at my previous appointment). I waited with at least forty other people, some of whom were standing because there weren't enough chairs. We formed a diverse group: white, black, Hispanic, Asian.

When my name was called, I was told to go to a classroom with a group of other people. When I politely inquired what the class was and how long it would take, the instructor replied that the class, on nutrition, would take "about an hour." I told her that I was a foster parent there to pick up the checks for my foster child, the implication being that I didn't feel it was necessary for me to take the class. She replied, coldly and firmly, that I could take it now or reschedule it for another time. I was pissed off but figured I had the time and we were out of formula at home. I could have just gone and bought the formula, but my more frugal side totaled the cost of two months' worth, and more importantly, when I could stand it, I was trying to do everything by the book—to have the real foster parent experience.

I sat in the class and, in defiance, read my magazine while the instructor played an eight-minute video on how to read the nutritional information on food labels. Each participant then had to choose a food item from a table and answer questions that the instructor posed. "How many servings are in that orange juice? How much Vitamin C does it contain?" Still feeling resentful, I chose the least nutritious item I could find, heavy cream. It had

sixteen servings and almost no nutritional benefit, with the exception of a little vitamin A.

The whole class took only about twenty minutes and I wondered why the instructor hadn't told me that from the start.
Maybe an hour class was required by some federal regulation. Or
maybe she didn't like my attitude and she was trying to make me
more compliant by coming across as strict. Afterward, I stood
in the waiting room, as all the seats were taken again. When my
name was called, I was given the checks and my card. I asked
where I should go to make the next appointment (I wondered if I
would be able to stand going back), and the worker mumbled in
an unfriendly voice, "Look on the back of your card." Welcome
to the world of government handouts, where appointments are
given, not mutually arranged.

I left the building wondering how other WIC recipients felt
about the experience. I thought about how I had tried to skip
the instruction because I didn't "need" it—I wasn't poor and I
wasn't getting these vouchers for myself. I wondered why the foster care agency couldn't get these checks and give them to me.
And, of course, it occurred to me that probably no one, poor
or not, wanted to go through the hassle of getting these checks.
The vouchers can be used only for specific food items, as I was to
find out later at the grocery store. I tried to imagine what possible benefit accrued from having to pick up the vouchers. It was
clear that there was an educational component, and I wondered
whether, over time, WIC recipients did learn something about
nutrition and if the information impacted their buying or eating habits, or whether this was information they already had or
simply weren't interested in.

Another time when I went to WIC, there was a video running about buying fruits and vegetables at the farmers' market.
The staff was handing out coupons for twenty dollars' worth of
produce at city markets with a pamphlet about how to prepare

the produce, and they were really encouraging. I felt awkward taking the coupons, as Cecilia was a little young to eat the food, but I didn't want to refuse them either. I rationalized taking them by thinking that we paid for her jarred food, as the program pays only for cereal and formula for children her age. WIC was kind of a complicated program for me. While it is important to help people have enough to eat, I don't think there is any shame in accepting help, and we were entitled to it on Cecilia's behalf, I felt somewhat fraudulent using this program. Also, while it is clearly important that people eat nutritiously, I didn't like the implication that just because I was a WIC recipient and possibly poor, I didn't know how to eat properly. And it was uncomfortable to be "force-taught" in order to receive the benefit.

Michael was the first to use our WIC checks. When he came back from the grocery store, he handed me our ID card and some remaining checks. He explained that it wasn't so simple to use them. At the store, he had collected all the items he planned to buy plus the specified number of cans of formula and gotten in the checkout line. When his turn at the register came, and with a long line behind him now, the cashier informed him that he needed to get the checks authorized and stamped at the office before he used them. She was kind enough to hold the line while he did this. At the manager's office, a man explained that although we had received checks for two months, the checks were dated and could be used for only one month's worth of formula at a time. So when Michael returned to the cashier, he had to ask that she hold half the cans aside to be returned.

Even as we learned the system and got better at using the checks, it wasn't always a smooth process. One time, I was at a local supermarket buying some infant formula and baby cereal. On a previous trip, I had noticed that infant cereal was now sold with formula and fruit mixed in, and I had chosen that, thinking it would be easier to fix and maybe a little tastier. When I got to the register this time with my regular items and my WIC items, the cashier told me I couldn't get that cereal because WIC pays only for the plain cereal.

Interestingly, the formula was the more expensive liquid kind. I had always bought the cheaper powered mix. I wondered if the WIC management thought the recipients weren't capable of mixing the powder with water properly or if the formula company that had negotiated this contract had somehow worked this in. Anyway, when I told the cashier I had gotten this same cereal before, I knew immediately that it was a losing battle. I was talking to a cashier whom I had seen a lot at this grocery store, a mature woman who seemed to know every other customer by name and handled her job with experience. I said again, "I have bought this same cereal before with WIC vouchers." She replied that it had been a mistake. I said I would be happy to pay the difference between the cost of the cereals. She said that was not allowed by WIC. She firmly but quietly suggested that I walk over to the manager's office, where I got the same story. Embarrassed and angry, I said, "Why don't you put a sign up so people will know what they can buy?" The manager replied, "They should have told you at the WIC office." Maybe they had, and I had forgotten.

When I got back to the cashier with the proper cereal, she noted that the juice, which I had also purchased before with WIC checks, was two ounces too large. In the moment of tension between us, I thought I might start to cry. Then she took the juice, slid it over the scanner, and said, "Next time, get a smaller size." I felt humiliated by this experience, the attention it had called to me, and the way I had to sort through my grocery items. The next time I went shopping, I went to another grocery store. To my surprise, it didn't accept WIC. When I related this to a friend, she said the store was "too upscale."

The Foster Care Stipend

Lenny Levinson, whose primary profession is writing, was a case-worker for several years at ACS and wrote an article that focused on the repetitive paperwork and bureaucratic waste there to the detriment of the children who are taken into care by New York City (Levinson 2000). By his calculations, the city spends about $62,000 per child per year. This is a lot of money, but I had my own interpretation—we received a stipend of about $6,000 per year. (The summer associates at Michael's law firm were earning almost this much every two weeks; I am not sure which fact is more shocking.) Our stipend, about one-tenth of the $62,000, was meant to house, feed, clothe, and pay for babysitting for Cecilia. I was providing all the care for less than what the U.S. Department of Agriculture estimates the average lowest-income two-parent household spends for the basic expenses of a child (Center for Nutrition Policy and Promotion 2005, ii). Like all foster parents I know, I paid any extra expenses myself.

Stipends increase as children age, as do expenses. Some foster parents receive higher special or exceptional stipends, depending on the level of care the children they care for require. The exceptional rate, the most paid per month, still comes to only $17,000 per year, and this for the care of children who have "physical and /or emotional and behavioral problems to the extent that if a foster family were not able to care for them, they could be institutionalized." The extra money in the higher stipend is intended for special transportation or equipment for the child. The agency handbook explicitly states that it is not a "wage payment" to foster parents, although I am sure the specialized care that these children need prevents most of their foster parents from working outside the home. And foster parents with children who receive the special or exceptional rate are required to take extra training each year.

Michael and I were asked numerous times by our friends and

acquaintances if we thought that many foster parents were "doing it for the money." (I think middle-class people sleep better when we assume that adults are being paid to care for children whom we as a society are responsible for.) We would first explain that there wasn't much money in foster care for foster parents, to which some people replied, "Yeah, but if they take in like ten kids?" And then we would patiently explain that taking in ten kids wasn't permitted. But for argument's sake, if one could take in ten kids, economize, and have a little left over, would it be worth it to have to live with ten kids?

A retired East Harlem couple described in a newspaper article typified the foster parents I got to know at my agency: In their fifties with three grown children, they decided their small house was too quiet. They have cared for fourteen children in two years and have now convinced their neighbor to take in children as well (Gittrich 2000). Of course, there are foster parents with poor intentions or just poor parenting skills. Occasionally I witnessed a foster parent at the agency speaking inappropriately to a child, and it made me cringe. But most of the people I met seemed very decent, and poor. They came to be foster parents for many reasons. One woman had been adopted herself and knew "what these kids go through"; another who had cared for children in foster care for twenty-eight years told me that her "heart ached for these children"; and a third, who wanted to adopt, took in a child who was unlikely to return to her parents.

The practice of reimbursing foster parents for some of the costs of caring for a child dates back more than one hundred years. Stipends were initially paid to discourage families from putting children to work to earn their keep. They were intentionally set at levels slightly lower than the cost of covering the child's expenses. The basic argument for the low level of reimbursement applies today: Foster parents have to want to foster for humanitarian reasons, not for profit. So the people who make the most significant difference in quality of life for the children in foster care, the foster parents, are the only ones *not* getting paid; who does get paid are lawyers, judges, social workers, and administrators. Because they are not employees, foster parents also forgo health insurance and Social Security benefits. Since the foster care system depends on career foster parents and children benefit from their experience, it is a shame that the system doesn't support and encourage these parents. And if children can't be cared for in foster homes (due to either a lack of homes or the child's difficult behavior), the next step for them is often a group home, which can cost two hundred dollars per day or more, depending on the level of care.

The stipend payment is a complicated issue. Many argue that birth parents would be doing a much better job themselves if they had enough money to pay for necessities for their children. After all, even the foster care stipend is more than any poor parent receives as a subsidy to raise their children. It is an important and valid point that children should not be removed from their families only because the families can't support even a basic subsistence-level lifestyle. It is certainly cheaper for the government to help an intact family financially than to pay for foster care. And it is far less traumatic for children to remain with their birth family. However, this gets back to what society feels comfortable paying for. It is easy for us to feel sorry for children separated from their parents but not so easy to sympathize with the parents. And, of course, there are some families that abuse or neglect their children, regardless of their income. Having said all that, stipend payments are really a separate issue: Foster parents do not have the same legal and moral obligations (and power) birth parents have, whether they feel this way or not. Foster parents are not adoptive parents. They are temporary caretakers with little control, and they should be paid for their work, or at a minimum be reimbursed for their actual expenses of caring for the children.

During a mandated training session at the agency, a foster par-

ent asked the instructor, an agency employee, what he looks for
in evaluating a potential foster family. Without identifying exactly
what criteria he used, the instructor proudly spoke about how he
weeds out parents "who are just in it for the money as opposed
to those who really want to help the kids." I cautiously asked,
"Why shouldn't foster parents expect to be paid for the valuable
work they do?" I pointed out that people in other professions
loved their jobs and still got paid for them. The social work intern (the only other white person in the room) spoke up and said
that as a social worker she would be paid a lot less than a doctor,
lawyer, or stockbroker. The instructor said, "Yeah, do you know
that as part of her internship, she is working here for nine months
for *free?*" The other foster parents met this with silence. I wanted
to stage a revolution. The student intern would end up with a
master's degree at the end of her training. She would be qualified
for a paying job. The foster parents, who worked every day, all day
(not twenty-one hours a week), regardless of their years of service,
would end up with almost nothing that was professionally useful.
I wish I had known what the other foster parents were thinking,
but I didn't, so I kept quiet.

We didn't resent paying for things for Cecilia. However, we
could afford to do so. We took in a child knowing that our lifestyle wouldn't change; we knew that we were comfortable covering the expenses of the two children we brought into the world.
However, there are many less selfish people, living closer to the
financial edge, who make real sacrifices (even on behalf of the
children they already are responsible for) to be foster parents.
Why should they have to do so?

Many foster parents are poor and uneducated. As with stay-at-
home mothers, the lack of pay contributes to their powerlessness
and diminished status. Foster parents have no rights as employees and aren't protected by any laws. If an accident happens in
their home and they are sued, they have no liability insurance or
employer to support them in the lawsuit. If children in a foster

parent's care destroy belongings in their home, it is at the discretion of the agency as to whether they will be reimbursed. Since they have volunteer status, foster parents can't join a union, and if they feel they are being treated unfairly, the formal grievance procedure is often uncertain.

Foster parents like children. They get involved with foster parenting to begin with because they feel that caring for children is important work, not because they want to be part of a big bureaucracy, and yet working with the system becomes an essential part of their volunteer position. Interacting with the foster care system often reminded me of dealing with the board of education when I needed to get specialized services for Peter, with one important difference. Even though the board of education was difficult and time consuming to work with, I had status and rights as Peter's parent. As an individual foster parent, you are expendable.

During the time that we were foster parents, I had an interesting point of comparison. A previous occupant of our house had requested information at one time from the adoption services arm of our agency, and mail for her continued to arrive from the agency after she had left. The invitations to training and seminars were politely written and sent in advance; in general, they sounded interesting and inviting. Letters to us about foster care training often were not. One letter we received on January 30 was dated January 26. Two sentences said that we should "be sure" to attend, while a third sentence reiterated the thought with "it is strongly suggested." However, all the training was for the month of February, half of it offered in the first week, making advance planning for it impossible. There are several differences between the group of people receiving letters about adoption and those receiving letters about foster care training from the same agency. The potential adopters were most likely white, middle class, and prepared to pay fees. The foster parents were most likely nonwhite and working class, as well as volunteers.

The results of a survey published in a child-welfare journal in-

dicated that foster parents have two primary suggestions to improve the child-welfare system: Show increased respect for the
individual caregiver, and provide concrete assistance and services.
One caregiver was quoted because her thoughts seemed to be representative of the group: "Please stop tying our hands behind our
back. . . . Let us be grown adults taking care of our kids and let
us use our own mind. Stop treating us like we were the child and
they [child-welfare caseworkers] were the adults" (O'Brien, Massat, and Gleeson 2001, 735).

When we became foster parents, people said to us, "I could never
do that, I would get too attached." Sometimes the comment
seemed intended as a compliment and meant that they thought
we were brave. But many times it also seemed to emphasize the
gulf between our circumstances and other parents; they separated
themselves from a world they didn't want to be part of, that when
they attached to a child, it was for good, in the normal way. And
it is true, foster care is an odd world. An enormous bureaucratic
system takes over the parenting responsibility of a child, so that
the child, in effect, has no permanent human family. The stigma
associated with the system is, in many ways, understandable and
maybe even healthy, in that the discomfort can be a motivation
for change.

Charles Loring Brace is largely considered the founder of the
modern foster care system. His belief that children were better off
raised in a family environment rather than in an institution or
group setting was novel in the mid–nineteenth century. Programs
like the Children's Aid Society, which Brace started, sent approximately 250,000 children from New York City to nonrelated families, many on Midwest farms, between 1854 and 1929. The children
were all poor, at a time "when the majority of upper-class Americans thought of poverty and criminality as more or less synonyms"

(O'Connor 2001, 30). The children were mostly born of immigrant parents, one or both of whom were alive, despite the tendency later on to refer to the transport of these children as "orphan trains." One of Brace's most significant contributions was respectful treatment of the children—he emphasized that they were not criminals, but products of their environments. He had "an abiding belief in the capability and fundamental goodness of poor city children" (298). Considering the stigma that we experienced and observed as foster parents and on behalf of our foster daughter, his beliefs do not seem to have permeated today's foster care system.

The media focus on the stereotypes of foster care, the horror stories of abuse, and not on the children who adapt and go on to live normal lives. An issue of *Time* had a cover story, "The Shame of Foster Care," with "Shame" spelled out in bright red letters (Roche 2000). Aside from its unfortunate title, which implied it was shameful to be *in* foster care, the story made a reader wonder if, considering the system it portrayed, children would in general be better off with their neglectful or abusive birth families. And although there are many who seem happy to criticize these "terrible" birth families, few seem to want to take responsibility for the children once they are without homes and families.

The internationally adopted child and the U.S. child in foster care present contrasting—and unfortunate—stereotypes. Although all these children come from arguably similar poverty-stricken circumstances, internationally adopted children are often portrayed as superior and more worthy of rescue. Even the families who take them in are differentiated in the media from foster families. Families who adopt internationally are portrayed as loving and desperate for a child, while foster families are portrayed as abusive and in it for the money. They are "bad by association" and have to fight the "shame" of being part of the system. This shame or stigma filters down to the children in care.

Part of the stigma of foster care is the notion that all the children in care are unhealthy. Once when I was visiting my sister, we went to an outlet mall twenty minutes outside Iowa City. We spent some time in the Carter's outlet getting some clothes for the children. A friendly older woman, a grandmotherly type, walked up to me and asked how Cecilia came to live with us. I told her that Cecilia was our foster daughter. I didn't mind the initial questions because I thought that the woman might be interested in becoming a foster parent. But when she asked if Cecilia was healthy, I felt offended. I was familiar with this assumption—that children in foster care (and maybe especially if they are black) are damaged in some way. I replied, "Doesn't she look healthy?"

Another time, I went to meet a babysitter who had put up notices offering child care in her home. I told her that since Cecilia was in foster care, I wasn't entirely sure how many months I would need a babysitter, but I would keep her informed as I heard the plans from the agency. After we met, I told her that I would like to think about the babysitting because she wanted me to commit to more hours than I wanted, and that I would call her the next day. When I did call, she said, "You know, I was talking to my husband and he reminded me that I forgot to ask if the baby has any health problems." I am sure she did not ask other parents about their children's "health problems." I had never been asked that question in regard to Martha or Peter. I said that Cecilia didn't have any health problems and that I didn't think the babysitting arrangement would work out.

In the first week of July, I attended training on shared parenting. Foster parents are required to attend ten hours of training per year. The agency takes a carrot-and-stick approach to persuade busy (or jaded) foster parents to attend. The foster care world doesn't use traditional incentives such as payment for your time or the opportunity to learn something valuable. Instead, free food (invariably bagels) and two subway tokens that are referred to as "carfare" are offered as incentives. The "sticks" are the threatening letters you receive when you don't put in the required hours. "Our records indicate that you are out of compliance with the training requirement to maintain your foster care license. You must attend the following training on Child Abuse and Discipline . . ."

Of the fifteen foster parents attending "Shared Parenting," I was the only white person and one of the least experienced—one woman had fostered for twenty-seven years, while others had fostered for fourteen and fifteen years. I had been looking forward to this training, thinking that it would help me come to terms with exactly what it promised—"shared parenting." I even had a concrete question: What do other foster parents have the children call them? Peter and Martha called us Mommy and Daddy. We referred to ourselves that way to Cecilia, to include her in our family, but we weren't sure if that was "right." In fact, our neighbor told us he thought it was wrong. The trainer had been brought in all the way from Nebraska, and therefore I assumed this training was going to be something special.

I was disappointed. The crux of the training was a discussion about the triangular roles of persecutor, victim, and rescuer—both within a family and in relation to the systems of foster families, birth families, and the agency. The trainer suggested that when foster families take the role of rescuer, they put the birth families in the role of persecutors or victims. The trainer wanted foster parents to work more closely with the birth parents. We were supposed to be more open to birth parents so we could mentor them.

In my small group, we ignored the role-playing assignment. When a foster parent started complaining that the agencies require much more from the foster parents than from the birth parents, others joined in: "How come all the rules is on us?" "Why don't the birth parents have to come to these trainings?" (Because we weren't part of the professional team, we weren't aware of the demands on the birth parents.) Swayed by the group, I suddenly didn't feel empathetic to the birth parents' situation—I felt put upon by the agency. Why did I have to spend four hours attending training I didn't need? I wasn't the one who had been found neglectful. At the moment, it occurred to me that perhaps it wasn't realistic to ask foster parents to attach themselves to the children in their care and at the same time to feel empathetic to the parents who have failed those children in some way. Although it wasn't one of the suggested training scenarios, ironically, we foster parents felt ourselves to be "victims," with the agency as our "persecutor."

There were two trainings I went to the first year that were interesting and informative, and where I felt I was treated as an adult: "Adopting through the Foster Care System" and "The Effects of Alcohol and Drug Abuse on Children." The first training wasn't something I thought I would ever need, but it was a subject I knew little about. The knowledgeable instructor was an attorney who handled adoptions through foster care. She explained that children become available for adoption in six different circumstances. First, parents can voluntarily surrender rights to a child, a quite unusual occurrence. Second, if parents abandon their child and have no contact with the child for six months, the parents' rights will be terminated. The last four reasons are situations in which parental rights are terminated due to a parent's abuse, neglect, mental illness, or mental retardation.

The training on parental use of alcohol and drugs and its effects on children was presented by the head of the Medical Department. The audience was about half staff and half foster parents, including one woman who attended with her daughter and referred to herself as a "foster grandma." It was particularly interesting because the trainer, a doctor, had been working for more than twenty years with children who had been exposed to drugs or alcohol in utero. Besides being knowledgeable, she was respectful and not at all condescending. We learned that many of the obvious effects of parental drug use on children can be remedied over time. Alcohol abuse is considered much more dangerous, often with lasting effects of hyperactivity and learning problems in school. We also learned that if a woman is using one drug, it is likely that she uses other substances—for instance, alcohol and nicotine—making it difficult to isolate the effects of different drugs. The doctor also spoke about how many children in foster care come from homes that aren't just poor but have a "poverty of environment."

One night, we went to dinner at a nice restaurant with some friends. Inevitably, the conversation turned to the baby. Our friends mentioned how lucky Cecilia was. I had heard this comment before, and I knew when people said this they were trying to flatter us. I think our friends were trying to say that we were a nurturing family and that a child would be happy with us, but sometimes these comments made me think about the unjustness of a world where some have so much, and others so little. Especially in that expensive restaurant, their words seemed to take on additional meaning. The implication seemed to be that this baby born to so little was "lucky" to have landed in a household that can afford to send children to private school. I asked myself: And Peter and Martha? Are they lucky too? Or are they deserving because they are white and our biological kin? I said that maybe Cecilia was born "unlucky," not being able to live safely with her birth family, but that we were trying to correct that by providing her with what she needs and deserves, like any other human being.

Our friends' next question was not one we had heard frequently: "Do you worry about the birth mother coming to your house to try and take advantage of you?" I was uncertain exactly how they envisioned her taking advantage of us, but I simply replied that most birth parents' lives are so devastated, they couldn't organize themselves enough to "take advantage." The question did make me think, though, about our feelings just six short months before about the birth family and our anxieties about meeting them. Despite my experience as a social worker, I had thought of a potential birth family as I thought of myself at some level, empowered and in control of my life. Now I could see so much more clearly that these families, so destitute, uneducated, often traumatized and disempowered by the system, are in no position to take advantage of anyone. A comment by Brenda Smith, the Australian social worker I mentioned earlier, describes this eloquently: "The feelings of low self-esteem attached to social deprivation are often further exacerbated by contact with the child-welfare system. Once children enter care, parents appear to internalize society's view of them, and are often unable to initiate and maintain contact with their children. Parents blame themselves rather than their circumstances" (Smith 1991, 176).

Shortly after our dinner out, I read an article in the *Wall Street Journal* about people stealing things when they don't need to. One of the choicest examples was a man who pays for economy tickets and then sneaks up to a first-class seat. He proudly stated in the interview that he had managed to steal a seat five or six times. The article seemed to say that such people were not meeting a *necessity* but seeking a thrill. As long as you steal for excitement and not from neediness, you remain socially acceptable.

4

I'm Vanilla, You're Chocolate

I WAS WALKING down the steps of our brownstone with Cecilia in my arms, taking her a few houses away to a baby-sitter while I went on an errand. It was a beautiful day and on my neighbor's steps sat Junior, a Jamaican American who had been doing some work next door for several weeks and with whom I had a nodding acquaintance. I often saw him on the steps reading his Bible during his breaks. As I walked past him after saying good-bye to Cecilia, he stopped me. "Excuse me. Can I tell you something? I've been watching that baby and, you know, she truly love you. I see the way she watches you and reaches out for you.

Note: The chapter title is a play on Marguerite A. Wright's title, *I'm Chocolate, You're Vanilla: Raising Healthy Black and Biracial Children in a Race-Conscious World.*

93

Just as natural as when my grandkids come to me." Junior bent
his knees and held out his arms, demonstrating how he reaches
for his grandchildren. "It doesn't matter that the colors of your
skin are different. Your blessings will come not from man but
from God himself."

With Cecilia's arrival, we began to evolve into a multicultural
family. We no longer felt just white. In most ways, our own changing cultural identity as a result of having Cecilia in our family
was liberating and wonderful. Initially, I thought a lot about how
people, both black and white, perceived us, and I worried about
how they would react to our caring for Cecilia. And then I went
through a period of feeling exuberant about the diversity of our
world. I fantasized about adopting children from all over the
world just so I could become closer to every culture and race. But
gradually the issue no longer seemed significant, because I was
wrapped up with my feelings for Cecilia as an individual and my
concerns about her future. After several months, race was more a
peripheral issue.

However, this change also made us vulnerable in a way that
we had not been before. We felt more personally sensitive to and
injured by racism. I wish I could say I had been as sensitive before
caring for Cecilia, but it was through our attachment to her that
we became vulnerable. It reminded me that when I got married
to Michael, I felt part Jewish. I had grown up knowing that there
was discrimination against Jewish people and here I was, attaching
myself to someone Jewish. This is extreme, but I thought, What if
there is another Holocaust?

When Michael and I had filled out the agency form for prospective foster parents, we had stated that we would take a child
of any race partly because we live in a diverse Brooklyn neighborhood where we thought any child would feel comfortable. Besides, we were offering to take in a very young child and therefore
it didn't seem race would be an issue. A young child would be

oblivious to color. While some children under the age of four may be able to identify differences in race and skin color and even label them, they are not aware of the meaning of the labels (Crumbley 1999).

While a very young child is "cultureless," in a sense, we did realize that taking care of a child that was born into another culture, whether or not the child had absorbed it yet, would be significant to us and our community. However, we saw this as an opportunity. We welcomed the idea of diversity and felt that it enriched our lives. And at some level, we felt that our experience melding our Jewish and Catholic backgrounds while raising a family might give us more insight. While a difference in religion is less obvious to strangers than is a difference in race, we had to go through some of the same thought processes any two people of different cultural backgrounds might. We thought of our families' reactions (for instance, Do you think your grandmother would have preferred that you had married someone who is Jewish?); we have to deal with people who oppose others marrying outside their religion; and we continually work on incorporating both our religious cultures into our children's lives.

Peter and Martha expressed honest feelings about taking in a child of a different race. Peter said that any race was fine with him but that he thought Asian babies were very cute. I think his comment reflected the plethora of adopted Asian children in our neighborhood. Martha was less certain; she was worried that other people would think the baby didn't belong to our family. I too worried about others' reactions.

When Cecilia arrived, I was caught up in the emotions of being a foster parent for the first time, an experience that was magnified because Cecilia was also the first nonwhite child I had ever cared for. As I got to know Cecilia over days and weeks, I began to see that her skin wasn't just brown, it was a deep mix of several rich tones. I would stroke her jet-black hair, which was a wonderful contrast to her skin and indescribably soft, like the feathers on a duckling. Sometimes as her little brown hand rested inside my larger white one, I was struck by the contrast in our skin tones.

The skin-tone contrast that I privately marveled over elicited dozens of comments. I had to think about racism and black and white cultures and how, even though we were just taking care of a baby who needed some temporary parents, we were a complicated picture that attracted a lot of attention. Even the Hispanic babysitter said that people stared at her when she took Cecilia out. One of the things I particularly worried about was that some black people might feel upset that we were parenting a black child. If I could have posted a sign on my back, it would have read: "We are trying to help a family get back together. We are foster parents. We aren't kidnapping this child." Part of my concern came from a vaguely remembered stance by the National Association of Black Social Workers (NABSW) that white adoption of black children was a form of cultural genocide. And of course, people on the street had no idea whether we were babysitters or foster or adoptive parents.

When I researched this, I found that in the early seventies, white parents were becoming increasingly interested in adopting black children. This surge of interest happened for a variety of reasons, including the decreasing number of white infants available for adoption as more and more single white women chose to keep their babies rather than give them up for adoption (Stein 1998). And of course, the civil rights movement had significantly impacted race relations in the United States, so that the idea of adopting a black child became for the first time for some white families an acceptable possibility. In response to this trend of white parents adopting black children, the NABSW issued this statement in 1972:

Black children should be placed only with Black families whether in foster care or adoption. Black children belong physically, psychologically and culturally in Black families in order that they receive the total sense of themselves and develop a sound projection of their future. Human beings are products of their environment and develop their sense of values, attitudes, and self-concepts within their own family structure. Black children in white homes are cut off from the healthy development of themselves as Black people. (Roberts 2000, 246)

The stridency of this statement was politically grounded in black nationalism, but it also reflected concern for African American families (Patton 2000, 3). It was perhaps too easy to draw parallels between transracial placements of African American children and the intentional destruction of other minority cultures through removing their children. Earlier in the century, Native American children in the United States and Aboriginal children in Australia were forcibly removed from their homes and communities and placed in Eurocentric environments in a deliberate attempt to destroy their birth culture.

The position of the NABSW had a significant effect on the adoption field. Not only was there a decrease in the number of transracial adoptive placements, but policies and practices in the various states were altered to require adoptive placements only with parents of the same race. However, while the impact on the adoption world was consequential, transracial placement continued for children in foster care.

A distant cousin told me a story that illustrated how placing children transracially in foster care but not in adoption could make for a very difficult situation. During the summer after Cecilia arrived, we went to a family reunion picnic where I met a woman named Heather, and we learned that our grandparents were first cousins. When I introduced Heather to Cecilia, she told me that her mother had taken in an African American infant through foster care in 1977. They had cared for the child for three years and wanted to adopt her, but the social service agency opposed the idea and returned the child to her birth mother. The birth mother was either unable or uninterested in caring for the child, because she promptly took the little girl to Florida and left her with her birth father, whom the child had never met. When I asked Heather why social services did not want her parents to adopt the child, she replied that one of the big issues was that social services didn't think Heather's family would be able to take care of the child's hair. It was unclear why social services hadn't worried about this issue for the first three years of the child's life. Heather's family hired a private detective to find the little girl in Florida, and the birth father willingly gave the child back to them. Heather's family raised the child, now twenty-two and in college, although she was never legally adopted.

In addition to concern that white parents cannot give a black child a healthy cultural identity, critics of transracial adoption suggest that white parents are unprepared to teach a minority child how to deal with racism. It has been said that because whites are not subjected to the same treatment as minorities in the United States, they are sometimes unprepared to identify racism, to respond to racism in a way that is least harmful to the child, or to teach a child to fend for himself (referred to as a "cultural survival kit"). Transracial adoption in the United States almost always means a white family taking in a nonwhite child, not a black family adopting a white child. However, this does not seem to be happening in significant numbers. The Child Welfare League of America conducted a survey of twenty-two states and found that only 4 percent of all adoptions of children in foster care in 1993 were transracial. The same year, another researcher found that among all adoptions, not just those that took place through foster care, only about 1 percent involved adoptions of African American children by Caucasian parents. It happens even less frequently that parents of color adopt a white child. However, in foster care, where many of the foster parents are black or Hispanic, white children are placed with nonwhite families in larger numbers, and occasionally these placements lead to adoption.

By 1994, the NABSW had modified its position with a three-tiered statement. The priority, the top tier, was preserving or re-unifying black families; the second tier was adoption by parents of the same race; and the third tier was adoption by parents of another race, but only after appropriate members of the African American community had determined that the second tier was unreachable (NABSW 1994). This model closely follows the federal legislation for placement of Native American children: The Indian Child Welfare Act prevents Native American children from being adopted outside the tribe without tribe oversight. While the NABSW modified its position, it also shifted focus. Rather than oppose adoptions that weren't happening in dramatic numbers anyway, the NABSW concentrated on another issue that had led to transracial adoptions: removing barriers that prevented African Americans from adopting in larger numbers.

Recognizing the importance to the child of the developed bond between caregiver and child in foster care placements, as have most researchers, the NABSW has stated that it is not against the transracial adoptions that sometimes follow foster care place-ments; in that situation the child's attachment needs would su-persede her need for cultural ties. It was difficult for me at first to form an opinion on the NABSW's position because I was so white oriented and I didn't know if it made sense from a black perspec-tive. Was this a radical position or a rational approach? Was it racist? It certainly made me uncomfortable.

I thought a lot about transracial placements in the first few months that Cecilia lived with us. During a home visit, I finally got my courage up to broach the subject just as the caseworker was about to leave. I paused with my hand on the doorknob.

"I am just curious. Does the agency allow transracial adoption?"

"Of course," he said. "This isn't the 1950s, you know."

I felt embarrassed having asked the question, but I was curious and I wasn't sure whom else to ask. I still felt then that I was tiptoeing around racial issues. I wasn't sure what I thought or whether I was offending people. The caseworker was Haitian, and his quick response made me question whether he fully understood white/black dynamics, at least as they pertained to policies on transracial adoption in the United States. His response sounded almost flippant—as if I had been sleeping for fifty years, unaware that everything had changed. However, even in the 1980s our foster care agency discouraged the adoption of black children by whites.

I soon found out that the caseworker was absolutely right about transracial placements of children in the year 2000. The Multi-Ethnic Placement Act (MEPA) of 1994 said that race could not be the determining factor when placing a child in an adoptive or foster home. However, the legislation did note that an agency could consider the capacity of the prospective foster or adoptive parents to meet the needs of a child of a different racial, ethnic, or cultural background as one of a number of factors used to determine the best interests of the child. Because MEPA is federal legislation, any state that receives federal money for its public or private foster and adoptive agencies (which is every state) must comply with it. And in 1996, the law was modified to make it even stricter. The Inter-Ethnic Placement Act, still commonly referred to as MEPA, said that race couldn't play any role in adoptive placements. In other words, the law says it is illegal to consider race when placing a child in a foster or adoptive home. So if a child is available for adoption and several couples are interested in the child, the couples that match the race of the child cannot be given preference on those grounds. Of course, a couple can refuse a placement if they aren't comfortable with a child of another race, even without explicitly saying that is the reason, but the child cannot (the exception would be an older child who might be able to express a preference). MEPA is a one-way street.

When Cecilia arrived, I didn't know anything about the practical aspects of caring for a nonwhite child. In fact, I knew so little that I didn't even know what I didn't know. For example, was skin care different for a black child than for a white child? I looked for advice anywhere and everywhere. After a checkup at the agency one day, I went to the waiting room to make the next appointment. A blond-haired, blue-eyed woman asked me how old Cecilia was. I told her four-and-a-half months, and when the woman commented on her size, I said, "Yes, she is big, and I think that may be one reason she is such a good sleeper." She responded—English was clearly this woman's second language—"I think black babies are very good!" She then told me she would fix Cecilia's hair by buying gel and two combs to part the hair to make small curls. I was struck by this encounter for many reasons. One was that this woman was only the second white foster parent I had met, and she was very friendly. I had tried making conversation with other foster parents but after three months, I didn't always feel warmly received and I wondered if they viewed me with suspicion because I was white. This may have been true or just paranoia on my part, because later, as I became more active in the agency, other foster parents did become friendlier. Another reason the encounter struck me was that although it seemed a little odd to have two white women talking about styling black hair, I was very happy to hear someone's advice.

Some of the things I wondered about were whether Cecilia's skin needed sunblock and how often her hair should be washed. I eventually learned the answers from books (for example, Kinard's *No Lye! The African American Woman's Guide to Natural Hair Care*) and friends, as well as from strangers in the drugstore. Many times

I bought hair and skin products either that didn't do what they were supposed to or that I didn't like (hair cream that was sickly sweet smelling or lotion that was too sticky). In the end, the best products I found were recommended by people who used the products themselves. And the new creams and conditioners were integrated into our family. Those of us with extra-dry skin use a heavy lotion, and those with curly hair use a conditioner that untangles the curls.

Many of the other issues related to race were much more complicated and not as neatly resolved. During the initial period when Cecilia lived with us and I became temporarily obsessed with race, I noticed every baby that "matched" her mother or father and every one that didn't. My eye was like a camera, and everywhere I went I took snapshots of children and their parents: white baby nursing at white mother's breast; Asian female face in a stroller with white male pushing the stroller; two brown parents with their two brown children. I was hyperaware of issues that I had thought a lot about before but that now seemed so personal. Christa Forman, a black high school senior adopted into a white family, wrote of her growing awareness of race, which had seemed inconsequential during her childhood: "Now, however, race is like a hurricane in my head crashing and thrashing about, leaving me feeling dizzy and confused" (Forman 2002, 21). She and I were in the same place.

Our situation triggered so many thoughts.

I thought about how others assumed that I was Cecilia's mother (in some capacity) and not her babysitter, although we live in a neighborhood filled with full-time babysitters. But these were mostly black babysitters caring for white children. This was part of my white privilege, the assumption that I was a mother and not a babysitter. A black friend who has a lighter-skinned baby confirmed my uncomfortable suspicion that people sometimes mistakenly assumed that she was her daughter's babysitter.

I thought about my own upbringing. Although my mother was not prejudiced and forbade any derogatory language in our house when I was growing up, our family did not live near or socialize with any black families. In fact, when I reflect on my childhood, it is amazing to me how segregated it was. I went to public high school in Albany, New York. Albany High is a large school; there were 2,700 students in my graduating class in 1982, and roughly 40 percent of the student population was black. Starting in the fourth grade, the classes were tracked by "aptitude." I was in the highest track, "academically talented" or AT. Three classes made up this tier, and I remember only one black student in the tier. This boy, Sam, was a bright and friendly guy, but I was aware of how he had to straddle the social gulf between the AT and the "lower"-level classes, where most of his real (black) friends were. Michael was a year ahead of me, and in his AT classes, there was one black girl. How had this school experience affected me as a developing person?

I don't know if it was during my time at Albany High that I began to wonder why no black students were in college-bound classes, or if it was earlier or later that I began to develop a social conscience and what I will call "white person's guilt." Although I knew that I had never personally hurt anyone based on race, I knew that I benefited from being white. I couldn't help wondering whether at some level I was a racist.

Now, as an adult, I was probably a fairly typical middle-class liberal white person trying to sort out my role or relationship to the child-welfare system, where there is a gross overrepresentation of black children. Whether it is the legacy of slavery, poverty, continued discrimination against blacks in the United States, or all of these factors intertwined that are responsible for the racial imbalance, the numbers are shocking. While African American children comprise approximately 17 percent of all children in New York State, they are the single largest group by race in foster care, at 44 percent. Comparatively, whites are 58 percent of the child population in New York State and 14 percent of the foster care population; Hispanics are 20 percent of the child population and 15 percent of the foster care population (Suleiman 2002). The overrepresentation of black children is even more astounding in large U.S. cities, where black children are often 80–95 percent of the foster care population.

These unfortunate numbers make it clear to me that black children are going to be placed in homes with foster or adoptive parents who are not black. There is no way that the black population could support that many children as foster and adoptive parents, although I often heard black women who were foster parents say, "These are *our* children, our responsibility." I felt differently; I felt all of society was responsible. These children are American citizens who have been removed (some youths formerly in foster care use the word "abducted") from their homes by our government. We have a collective responsibility and a moral obligation to ensure that these children find a safe and permanent place to live.

The NABSW statement clarifies that the real battles in adoption are for black infants and toddlers, who are wanted by both black and white couples. There are fewer white couples interested in adopting older or handicapped black children, thousands of whom linger in foster care waiting to be adopted. And of course, foster parents are always in demand. The NABSW statement also criticizes the lack of targeted outreach to the black community as foster and adoptive parent resources, as well as the inadequate supports to help black families stay together in the first place.

As I have pointed out, when your child is of a different race, you attract attention. I sometimes wondered about the effects of the attention to our racial differences on a developing child, even when the attention was positive and well intentioned. Everyone in our neighborhood seemed to know Cecilia's name and to pay attention to her. This seemed to be a nice thing for Cecilia, but when we were outside of our neighborhood, I was less certain. For example, when we were in Iowa visiting my sister, we were out for lunch and our waitress, exuding Midwestern charm, was very solicitous toward Cecilia. She brought some applesauce for her while we waited for our lunch to be served. At the end of our meal, she said, "I hope you don't mind me asking, but is your daughter adopted?" I responded that we were her foster parents. Her eyes lit up at my response, and she told me how her two children were in high school now and she had always thought of doing foster care. She then asked about our experience.

While it was hard to say whether Cecilia was too young to notice or be negatively affected by the attention, Peter and Martha definitely did find it annoying and embarrassing at times. I also quickly learned that when we were in public places, I had to keep my hand on the stroller or the grocery cart. If I didn't, people would look around, trying to identify Cecilia's mother, thinking that she had been abandoned. I had to clarify my relationship to Cecilia as her caretaker.

Sometimes the attention we attracted was interesting or amusing. For Martha's seventh birthday in June, we took a small group of children to Chelsea Piers, an enormous sports complex on Manhattan's West Side with an interior gymnastics and rock-climbing space. Michael and I took turns watching Cecilia and supervising the party. During my watch, a small group of adults passed and commented on what a lovely baby Cecilia was—and how tall my husband must be (they didn't mention, and brown). I was intrigued that they assumed we were biologically connected and pleased with myself that I could accept the comment without offering them any information. During Michael's turn watching Cecilia, he sat chatting with my brother-in-law, and again got the "lovely baby" comments, as well as "What proud dads you must be!"

Children's comments were often especially amusing, sometimes

because they were so blissfully unaware of the prejudice and stereotypes in our world. One day, my four-year-old nephew Andrew spread his hands on the pregnant belly of his Aunt Audrey.
"I looove that baby," he said. "Do you think it will be brown or
white?" Another time we went to Cooperstown, where I was born,
for a week. My sister and her husband had bought a vacation
home there and had joined the country club that we had belonged
to almost thirty years earlier. It is a beautiful place, green and
pristine, with a sandy beach along Otsego Lake. It looked exactly
as I remembered it, including the white, preppy people, many of
whom were from families I had played with as a child. Unlike the
city, where people sometimes mentioned our difference in race, no
one in Cooperstown spoke of it. They were color-blind—with one
exception. On the beach, a boy about eight years old who seemed
cognitively immature for his age pointed to Cecilia and asked
whose baby she was. I said she was mine. "But she is brown," he
replied. "Yes," I said, "she was born from a brown woman's body."
His mother looked mortified and tried to hush him up.

I have a casual friend, Deborah, who is white and whose son,
adopted from South America, is brown. About two months after
Cecilia came to live with us, Deborah asked me whether I had
experienced any racist incidents. It was an interesting question for
me because this was something I worried about anytime I took
Cecilia out of our neighborhood (and especially when I left New
York City). I tried to think through how I would respond to a
racist comment, but I felt totally unprepared.

At this early juncture, I was happy to tell Deborah, "Not
really." Deborah replied, "Well, unfortunately, you will. Racism
is subtle but persistent in our culture." She said one time she was
unloading her car, which was parked on the street, and her four-
year-old son picked up his backpack. A woman passing by came

over to her and said, "That boy is taking your backpack." I was a bit shocked and didn't want to believe anything like this might happen to us, but months later, I learned Deborah was right.

When I think of Deborah's words—"subtle yet persistent"— they bring to mind my experience with the book *What to Expect the First Year*. This is a highly respected book on child care and I used it extensively when Peter and Martha were infants. After a six-year baby hiatus, I consulted my copy again when I had questions about caring for Cecilia. It dawned on me that the book was written for parents of white infants, which had never occurred to me. For instance, the question "How do I care for my baby's hair?" was obviously directed at parents of white children, even though the authors didn't write, "For white children, this is what you do." Nor did they address what to do for children who aren't white. The assumption was that the reader was white. It was a disappointing but enlightening moment for me.

Fortunately my worries about having a confrontation with someone over some racist remark were unfounded. However, I did have two minor racist incidents. As we were driving from Chicago, where we had spent a few days sightseeing, to Iowa City, we stopped for lunch in Tampico, Illinois, the birthplace of Ronald Reagan. We took two tables next to each other and ordered what turned out to be a delicious lunch. During the meal, I noticed a white man staring at us and especially at me holding the baby. His stare was unabating and as I got up to go to the restroom, I took pleasure in returning it. Another time, a black grocery store clerk pointedly looked from me to the baby and back to me and rolled her eyes in an exaggerated fashion.

We did experience many stereotyped comments. When white people looked at Cecilia, still an infant, and suggested that she would be a good basketball player or said that she had "music in her blood," it emphasized the racial divide between whites and blacks. Those comments suggested to me that whites could not see a black infant as an individual with varying talents and interests. Cecilia was stereotyped into a group because the people who made those comments didn't know enough black people to think of blacks as individuals.

Occasionally we had an encounter where there was some stigma evident, but it was difficult for us to decipher if it had to do with racism or foster care. As Cecilia developed and it became evident that she was a bright baby, a few people commented, "She seems very clever—but she wasn't that way when you first got her, was she?" Since it is difficult to measure the intellectual capacity of a five-week-old, I am uncertain exactly what the point of these comments was. One has to try and not overreact, but such comments did not imply, "Wow, she is really blossoming." Michael and I both got the sense that people were implying that somehow our "whiteness" or class and all its benefits was rubbing off on her. The meaning was difficult to measure or interpret or understand precisely, but these comments came from white people (and to be fair, a small number). Comments from blacks about Cecilia were uniformly optimistic and flattering—they reflected confidence in Cecilia and her development. Perhaps African Americans, who are more accustomed to being misjudged, are more sensitive to stereotyping a person in circumstances that don't really reflect anything meaningful about that person.

What was stated at the policy level by the NABSW did not impact our day-to-day experience with black people we knew or met. We had only positive experiences with the black community. It may be that people were just polite or didn't feel comfortable telling us that they disapproved of us caring for a black child. It could also be that as a minority culture blacks regularly interact with the majority culture, so they are more comfortable or accepting of our situation, whether or not they feel comfortable with what the NABSW states on a policy level (assuming that the average black person is even aware of the policy).

The following was a typical encounter with a foster mother who was African American in the elevator one day after a visit to the agency. I introduced Peter, Martha, Cecilia, and my nephew, Harry, and she introduced the eight-year-old girl and ten-month-old boy in her care. She said that they came to her through foster care but that she planned to adopt them. She said that she does foster care for the "love of the children" and that there are too many children in need. She then said: "If you don't mind me saying so—I think it is wonderful that you have taken a black child in your home. And nice for them as well." She nodded toward Harry, Peter, and Martha.

We felt welcomed by the black community as Cecilia's caretakers. On the subway, on the street, in stores and restaurants, black women and men would start chatting with me or remark, "She is so cute!" One day, a woman asked how old Cecilia was and told me that Cecilia looked so much like her daughter at the same age. And I think that was a big piece of it: Cecilia might look like a black person's daughter, niece, or sister—a familiarity that they wouldn't feel if she were a white baby—and it is an opening for a short conversation. To some degree, I have noticed a similar phenomenon myself. To many people (including Jewish people), I look Jewish, and I have noticed a certain comfort emanating from many Jewish people in my presence. While I always say that I am not Jewish, it doesn't seem to matter—the comfort remains.

One time on an airplane, I sat next to an African American woman who told me a hilarious story about the weekend she had just spent in New Orleans with a very annoying friend. As I sat listening and laughing, I wondered if I would be having this conversation if I didn't have Cecilia with me. It wasn't just the friendly tone of our conversation—there was an almost immediate intimacy. Was I more open to friendships with black people or was I (because of my association with Cecilia) more welcomed or less threatening?

One Sunday during the summer while Peter and Martha were visiting their grandparents, Michael and I went to the Jewish Museum in lower Manhattan with Cecilia. We got on the F train and there was a black woman, very nicely dressed in a peach suit, who was preaching loudly. Cecilia craned her head around in her stroller to get a good look at her. When we got off the F to switch to the A train, the woman got off as well and sat next to us. Cecilia just couldn't take her eyes off her. The woman asked Cecilia's age and so on (the pleasant preliminaries) and then asked if we were babysitting for the day (the first person ever to ask us that question).

I told her that we were foster parents and she responded, "How nice, especially for a child of another race." She added, "Some people only care about people of their own race." Her comments affected me in a profound way. She was so right. She then went on to say that she was from Belize and that she had never really known any Chinese people there but since she has lived here, she realizes that they are the same as everyone else. She also mentioned that her neighbor had once taken in some white children in foster care.

Our initial anxiety about black people's reaction to us caring for a black child stemmed from the weight of history in this country that leaves some whites privileged and feeling guilty. And in fact, sometimes my worry stemmed from a feeling that, by caring for Cecilia, somehow we had taken advantage of or stolen something precious from black people as a whole. Although we were anxious ourselves, Michael and I were amazed at the number of white people who asked us whether we had encountered black people who were angry. I had not realized how universal this fear was. Somehow the NABSW statement from 1972 and the attitude behind that statement had made a clear and lasting impact on the white middle class.

Interestingly, in my experience, the more recent MEPA legislation, which prevented the consideration of race in foster care or adoption placement, was virtually unknown, even to lawyers. As was the 1994 NABSW position statement which doesn't say that only black children's culture should be protected. It says that *all* children should have a right to be raised within their own race and culture. Although the number of children adopted from other countries by Americans has risen dramatically in recent years (to roughly twenty thousand per year), I have never heard an analogous discussion about separating other children from their birth cultures.

Eventually, I began to feel that at some level white people's concern about how blacks feel about whites taking care of black children could also be an excuse for not getting involved with the black community. For example, it is hard to understand why in the year 2001, more Americans adopted children from each of three countries—China, Russia, and South Korea (4,681, 4,279, and 1,770 respectively)—than from Haiti, Ethiopia, Jamaica, and Liberia combined (452 children total) (Holt International 2002). At the same time, Canadians, Australians, and others privately adopt healthy black infants from the United States, making this country the only industrialized nation to place children outside its borders.

As Cecilia was growing and changing, so was I. In the first eight months I thought about race all the time. This was an eye-opening period. I began to see how "white" I was and how separated blacks and whites are in the United States. Almost since the moment the baby came to live with us, I started paying more attention to articles in the media about race—things I might have read before but that suddenly took on a more personal significance. The first week Cecilia lived with us there was an article in the newspaper about black women's performance in college. It was a story that I might have skimmed previously but that I now felt obliged and interested to read. And when I went to the nail salon, I no longer automatically picked up *Vogue* or *Mademoiselle*. I read *Honey* or *Essence* instead.

I also thought about things like why most of the faces of the Playmobile toy people are white. When my friend Deborah warned me about the racism we would encounter, she also mentioned that she had been dismayed by the lack of brown faces in books and toys. Deborah said that when her son was younger, she would color in the faces of the people in the books so that he could see brown faces as well. This seemed a bit extreme to me, but it did make me think. Was this really necessary for the child? I wondered. Would it matter to him or was it just his mother's issue? However, in time, I too began to notice the white faces on dolls, on toys, in books, and on patterned clothing. I never colored in any faces in a book but I decided that white culture was already well represented in our house, and I stopped buying any children's things that didn't represent a more diverse picture. I noticed and came to appreciate that our local drugstore carried greeting cards picturing families that are not white.

I became more aware of and interested in reading about serious issues from a black perspective, such as slave reparations. We needed to become more knowledgeable about issues that affected African Americans because that was our responsibility as Cecilia's caretakers. It didn't matter that she was being socialized in a white family because she would be identified as African American. While in some ways that need to become more knowledgeable was an additional responsibility in our already complicated lives, it was also very different from randomly selecting a culture to learn about. I have always had a general interest in culture and people around me. But when we became the caretakers of an African American child, our interest was focused and self-interested because we felt connected to African Americans through Cecilia.

In a series the *New York Times* ran on race in the United States, the articles indicated that relations have improved between blacks and whites but that race is still an enormous issue (see Correspondents 2001). One of the reporters working on the series said that sometimes he got tired of thinking about it, that is, of asking himself, Is this a racial moment? I understood what he meant. I would wonder, Is this person staring at me because she disapproves and is rude or is she just staring at my shirt wondering where I bought it? I read in one of the articles about how blacks and whites are isolated from each other and I thought this was very true. I thought about how having Cecilia in our home helped us break free from the isolation—both in our interactions with a black person on a very intimate basis that normalized our unconscious feelings about race, and with the outside world. At a certain point in the first year, I realized that I never thought about whether I was "racist" anymore. I knew I wasn't.

If one looks to research to guide decisions on transracial placements, one finds studies that look at the "well-being" of adults who since infancy (to eliminate possible confusion with issues that have to do with attachment) have grown up in a home whose culture differs from their birth culture. Researchers have tried to compare how happy and well-adjusted these adult adoptees are in contrast to the general adopted population. For example, research has looked at whether these transracially adopted adults get married or sustain permanent relationships with others at the same rates as other adoptees do. The well-being of transracially adopted children has been hotly contested. In a review of the literature on this topic, Madelyn Freundlich writes that, "in general, studies demonstrate no significant differences between children adopted in-racially and transracially with regard to overall well-being," despite criticism of some of the studies because of small sample size, among other issues (Freundlich 200b, 16–17).

In spite of our "liberation and enlightenment," Michael and

I were still two white people who had been raised in all-white environments. Although no one directly questioned our qualifications, we were asked many times by blacks and whites, "Who does her hair?" I sometimes wondered if this question was code for whether a white person can adequately care for a black child. And it seemed a legitimate question, starting with hair, skin, and health care right on to preparation for racism and pride in African American culture. In her book *Hair Matters*, Ingrid Banks notes that "hair meanings, in most cases, are specific to individual cultures; . . . scholars focusing on blacks and hair emphasize the importance of hair among blacks in relationship to Africa, constructions of race, enslavement, skin color, self-esteem, ritual, esthetics, appropriate grooming practices, images of beauty, politics, identity, and the intersection of races and gender" (Banks 2000, 6–7). If I think of my experience with Caucasian hair and how my knowledge reflects white (Northeastern) culture, I couldn't begin to try and teach somebody what I know. And even if I could, they would have only my perspective, not that of my mother, grandmother, aunts, sisters, and all the "white" homes I have been in over decades.

We weren't ideal candidates to raise an African American child despite our connection to and appreciation for many aspects of black culture. One night I had a dream that illustrated one aspect of this. I dreamt that I was in a fancy hotel and a wealthy white woman and her white attendant were speaking between themselves. I couldn't understand what they were saying but I felt that it was racist in some way. As the white women walked away, a black woman came in to clean the room. (I am embarrassed to admit this was her role, but that is how I dreamt it.) She turned to me as if reading my thoughts and said, "That's right, those comments were racist." I spent the rest of the dream trying to find the women so that I could tell them how I felt their comments were wrong. It was a depressing dream, because it felt as if not only would I not be able to respond appropriately but I wouldn't even be able to pick up on or interpret racist comments accurately.

It puzzled me to think that anyone could imagine that a child wasn't better off with a family that had at least one parent from the same race. At the very least, this would protect the child from constantly being identified as adopted. When I was asked through the months what would happen to Cecilia, I mentioned that if she wasn't able to return to her birth mother or go to live with a sibling, we wanted her to be placed with a black family. People seemed surprised. "But you are good parents," they would say. Yes, but Michael and I felt that life would be easier for Cecilia in a family of the same race. This is not to say that I am opposed to transracial placements, but when one considers all the options from the child's perspective, race is a significant factor in our society. Regardless of my personal conclusions, federal law says that race is irrelevant. It may not seem important to a couple desperate to adopt a child, but the truth is that race is extremely relevant. The NABSW (1994, 8) states that "it is through culture that we assign the meaning to circumstances, situations, and experiences in our world." Moreover, the statement notes, adding transracial issues to adoption exacerbates an already complicated situation.

I once had a discussion with an uncle who commented that he could understand how some Jewish people oppose intermarriage because of the history of persecution and the "specialness" of the Jewish culture. I was familiar with this topic and knew that the term "cultural genocide" was used here as well. I replied that all cultures were special. It is thought-provoking that the NABSW's policy statement is disregarded on a national level, especially considering the vulnerability of developing children, while disapproval of intermarriage of adults (who have already formed their identity) can be viewed as a rational attitude.

Part of our preference to have Cecilia raised by black parents had to do with our concern with how she would be accepted in the black community as an adolescent and adult. While in a financial management training program at the Equitable, my first big job after college, I met Kim, who one day asked me, "What do you think I am?" I knew what she meant, but I was speechless because, first, I wasn't used to having conversations about race with people I didn't know well; second, I wasn't sure; and third, I didn't want to offend her by giving the wrong answer.

After some hemming and hawing, I hesitantly said, "Hispanic?"

"No," she said, "my mother is German and my father is half black and half Native American."

"Wow!" I said. The conversation that followed was about her difficulty growing up as a mixed-race person in Queens. She said she never felt completely accepted by whites or blacks. I lacked the experience or maturity to hold up my end of the conversation, but I found it incredible that she didn't feel accepted wholly by any group. I was very naïve. The experience made me worry about what would happen for Cecilia if she weren't raised by African Americans. While she would never appear physically to be of mixed race, if white people raised her, in a sense she would be "mixed." Ruth McRoy (1999; 685) writes:

> White foster parents may seek to adopt African American infants and toddlers to whom they have become attached while temporarily caring for them. The child's appearance is often secondary to the fact that the family is strongly attached to the child. In some of these families, the children are noticeably different from the family in terms of skin color and hair texture, yet the family adopts a colorblind attitude and often seems oblivious to the hierarchy of physical features that can influence social status and treatment [inracially and transracially].

While I was initially confused and intimidated by the NABSW's statements concerning transracial placements, I came to understand what the organization was stating and why. I am not saying that transracial adoption is wrong or shouldn't happen, but all other things being equal, it is hard to argue that it is in a child's best interest (especially because a child who doesn't "match" his family is often asked why and loses a basic right to privacy.) The problem is that all other things will never be equal. Even at the individual family level, it is impossible to measure the quality of one family over another, especially when trying to consider the unique characteristics and needs of any child, which develop only over time.

Attachment: Meeting the
Eyes of Love

A child forsaken, waking suddenly,
Whose gaze afeard on all things doth rove,
And seeth only that it cannot see
The meeting eyes of love.

—GEORGE ELIOT, MIDDLEMARCH

T HE DEVELOPMENT of an attachment is like watching a living thing grow—it is almost impossible to see the growth, but a day or a month later, the evidence is there. The format of this chapter reflects the nature of attachment, which happens in immediate present-tense encounters. The idea of attachment and exactly when and how it happens is so elusive that I wanted to describe these months in the smallest possible bits of time so that the reader could get a sense of what happened. I have added some relevant excerpts from the professional literature to give context to our personal experience.

March 13, 2000 (approximately two weeks after Cecilia arrived)

Nelly, our former next-door neighbor from Brussels, is visiting. Today I took her to Brooklyn Heights to meet up with Katherine, another friend who had also lived in Brussels, for lunch. At least Nelly had a chance to speak in French with someone else, giving me a break, and Katherine had a chance to practice. Anyway, Katherine had her baby on March 1, a boy, Charlie. I brought him a little striped green cotton jacket for a gift. I had bought the same one for Cecilia in orange and red. Katherine met Cecilia for the first time and I met Charlie. He was so small still, just under two weeks. Katherine and I were almost gawking at each other, intrigued with our similar but different situations. She wanted to know what it was like to be a foster mother to an infant and I had a hard time putting the experience into words. "Fun" seemed a bit simplistic, but it was fun and somewhat confusing. At Katherine's, I noted the pleasant chaos of a house with a newborn. Ordinary life had obviously stopped for a few weeks with Charlie's arrival. In contrast, our house was more functioning: No maternity leave or extended visits from relatives for me. I knew what it was like for her, having given birth two times, but seeing her with Charlie made it very fresh in my mind. I thought about whether I wished that I was Katherine, with a newborn who was mine to keep forever. Maybe a little, but not really. That is why we chose to become foster parents, not adoptive parents. If we had wanted another child, we could have given birth to one. This is more complicated, caring for a child temporarily, but it is interesting.

Historically, foster parents have been viewed as temporary caregivers—or "babysitters"—for children in foster care. Children generally have been placed and removed from foster parents' care with little regard to the caregivers' rights or feelings about the children. Traditionally, foster parents were not considered as potential adoptive parents for the children for whom they were caring, even when the children had deeply bonded with them. In the 1980s, however, foster parents began to be viewed as more integral to the planning for the children whom they were fostering. With the emphasis on permanency for children, agencies began to ask foster parents to become more involved with the children's birthparents and more frequently sought them out as adoptive parents for the children being fostered. Nonetheless, agencies typically have not clearly defined the roles that foster parents were expected to play and, to the extent that foster parents have been asked to take on new responsibilities, often have offered little training or support. (Barbell and Freundlich, 2001, 35)

March 31

We had a fabulous time in Hungary. It is funny how the four days stretched out to seem like two weeks. It was great having Cecilia with us—somehow it seemed so much more natural than at home. We were free from our lives in New York and the agency and her birth family. The crib that the hotel provided seemed so big and cold. We had Cecilia sleep in our bed between us and she seemed to sleep so happily and soundly there. She sleeps well at home in her bassinet beside our bed but I think we hesitate to sleep with her in New York because it seems so personal. Infants are such intimate creatures in a way, happiest when they are snuggled as close as possible. While Cecilia sleeps in our arms all the time, I have hesitated to put her in our bed at all. Partly because she sleeps well independently and because it would seem cruel for her to get used to sleeping in a bed and then have her move to live with her sister, where she most likely would sleep in a crib. Also I don't think the agency would approve, even if it made Cecilia happy and secure. What are the foster parent boundaries?

The foster care system is characterized by a temporary nature with which most foster parents must come to terms. The impermanence of a family member alters many perspectives. How fully a family incorporates a child into its family system may be affected largely by its members' abilities to deal with the uncertainties of the child's placement. The foster family must struggle between the opposite poles of not including the child enough, or including the child so completely that the child's departure is extremely difficult for both. This difficulty extends beyond physical inclusion to the psychological inclusion or exclusion of the child in relation to the family. (Urquhart 1989, 194)

April 20
Today I spoke to Deborah, a friend with an adopted child and a birth child, on the telephone. She asked me about my attachment to the baby and how it was different from my first two birth children. I said that I was unsure— sometimes it seems the same and sometimes I feel less attached (I thought, "How does one know if one is attached?"). When I gave birth, I didn't think about attachment—I chose to have children, and caring for the infants was my responsibility. If Michael and I didn't care for them, who would? Of course, we grew to love each of our children deeply, but before we knew them as individuals, we cared for them because we were their parents. Attachment was almost beside the point. Deborah confidently stated that any hesitation on my part had to do with the nature of the foster care relationship. She said that I was protecting myself because my relationship with Cecilia was temporary. I wondered how she could know; she seemed to be so confident where I was so tentative.

I am just beginning to understand the planning system in foster care. As a backlash to the years that children used to spend

(and sometimes still do) in foster care, there has been a movement to accelerate the planning process. The new system is called
"concurrent planning." This means that when a child enters foster
care, a plan A and a plan B are developed. Plan A would always be
that the child would return to her birth family (unless they have
abandoned the child or committed some heinous crime). However, rather than wait for months to pass while the birth parents
are either getting it together or not, and *then* coming up with an
alternative plan, concurrent planning requires that plan B already
be in place. Often plan B involves the foster parents adopting the
child. This is a real shift, because previously foster parents were
discouraged from adopting, often because agency administrators
wanted those foster parents to remain available to take in other
children. In Cecilia's situation, plan B would be for her to live
with her half sister in another foster home, once another child
moved home and space opened up, although it was unclear to me
whether that would be Cecilia's permanent placement. I guess we
would be considered pre–plan B.

I am just beginning to realize the impossibility of the situation
we have gotten ourselves into.

In a paper delivered sometime in the 1930s, Clara Comstock,
one of the most hardworking and beloved of all placement
agents, recounted with clear pride how she used to trick people
into becoming foster parents. In one case she asked a couple
who had expressed interest in taking children to babysit a child
for just one night—ostensibly because the child had no other
place to stay. Then, the following morning, while the couple
was still under the spell of the child's cuteness and pathetic
fate, she rushed in, got them to sign placement forms, then
rushed out again before they had time to change their minds.
(O'Connor 2001, 304)

May

One evening this week, I was playing with Cecilia who was lying on her back on our couch. Peter was sitting on the stool to my side. I was talking to her and I said, "What are you so smiley about?" And Peter answered, "She's happy Mommy is home." His matter of fact tone, which contrasted with my uncertainty (Am I her mommy?), struck me.

Time is passing and I think about other older children in foster care and how this time affects their sense of self. Months must seem like years for these children. I wonder how it affects their attachment to their birth families and to their foster families. I always feel thankful that Cecilia is a baby so that she is unaware of her circumstances. And I wonder how the time and tenuousness of the bond affects the foster parents. An article about premature babies and the difficulty the parents sometimes have in their initial attachment because of the child's fragile medical state mentioned anticipatory grief. Anticipatory grief is when the parents are afraid of getting too attached to the baby (consciously or unconsciously) because they are afraid something might happen to the baby. I wonder how many foster parents suffer from anticipatory grief from never knowing how long the child will be with them.

June

Harry, my six-year-old nephew, is here to stay with us for two weeks. I took all four children with me for tonight's visit at the agency. As an incentive to Peter and Martha to cooperate, I told them that I would take them to McDonald's for dinner. Harry didn't seem to care too much about going to McDonald's but he was excited about taking the subway to Manhattan from Brooklyn. It was nice to have a child along who considered the ride a real treat.

When we got to the waiting room at the agency, two of Cecilia's older half sisters were already there. It was interesting to see Peter,

Martha, and Harry completely quiet on my left, eyeing the girls to my right—with Cecilia smack in the middle. I wondered what they were all thinking. The two sisters hung on the stroller saying hello to Cecilia, who pouted several times and then began to cry. I wondered if it was too much noise and activity for her or whether she realized that I would be leaving her. I noticed that Cecilia cried less and seemed happier at a visit recently with her mother and grandmother where only one of her sisters was there. Cecilia seems so smart, and I think she knows her sisters and knew that I would be leaving her. It really makes me feel bad to put her in a situation that seems stressful to her. If I had any choice in the matter, I would never leave her alone at the agency—it is contrary to my mothering instincts. I want to know what it is that makes Cecilia cry during the visits so that we can fix it, but no one seems to welcome my intervening. I think how Cecilia's crying must be stressful for her mother and her siblings.

> Attachment is the base upon which emotional health, social relationships, and one's world view are built; . . . [it] is a process. It takes time. The key to its formation is trust, and trust becomes secure only after repeated testing. Normal attachment takes a couple of years of cycling through mutually positive interactions. The child learns that he is loved, and can love in return. The parents give love, and learn that the child loves them. The child learns to trust that his needs will be met in a consistent and nurturing manner, and that he "belongs" to his family, and they to him. Positive interaction. Trust. Claiming. Reciprocity (the mutual meeting of needs, give and take). These must be consistently present for an extended period of time for healthy, secure attachment to take place. It is through these elements that a child learns how to love and how to accept love. (Becker-Weidman 2001, 34–35)

June 21

Cecilia had a checkup today at the agency. When I arrived, her mother was already there. As I was supposed to do, I had encouraged her to come and had made sure that she had the date and time. And yet when I saw her, I felt surprised—somewhat happy because Zuri was doing what she was supposed to do and somewhat sorry because it made the appointment more stressful for me. I still have not mastered the art of support to the parents while developing my own bond with the baby. I like the birth mother and feel sorry about her situation, but I couldn't imagine a more awkward circumstance under which to develop a relationship. After our hellos, I offered her the stroller to push back to the appointment room. It was kind of a funny gesture, a symbolic shift in power—handing over the reins to the "real" mother. During the appointment, Zuri was very sweet with Cecilia, softly singing her a song and rubbing her feet gently but the baby cried for me. With my heart wrenching, I encouraged her mother and tried to ignore the cries. I picked Cecilia up periodically to calm her but it was incredibly stressful and awkward. I felt that I was less soothing than I would be normally because I felt embarrassed that Cecilia's mother should have to see the intimacy of my relationship with her daughter. After the appointment, we walked to the subway together. She carried Cecilia, who had calmed down, in her arms. As we parted, she placed Cecilia in my arms and my heart went out to her as she walked away empty-handed. But it wasn't the same as what I felt when Cecilia cried during the appointment. That was torture. I feel that I have accepted Cecilia's attention, her smiles, her sweetness, her infancy that she will only experience once in her lifetime and that I owe her something in return. While babies will seek attention from almost everyone, they will light up for a few special people and you know when you are one of them. It is a gift that you accept from them—a gift with an obligation to love and protect them. Maybe that is attachment.

Only later, after the age of four to six months, does the baby seem to prefer Mother (or other significant caretaker) to anyone else, especially in times of stress. This is the key to our notion of attachment: the baby seeks out the attachment figure as a source of comfort when he is upset. And for babies who were adopted in the first month or so of life, "Mother" is defined not as the woman whose voice was overheard in the womb, but as the woman who did all the responding and diapering and feeding and cooing——the adoptive mother. (Brodzinsky, Schechter, and Marantz Henig 1992, 34)

These are a birth mother's thoughts on seeing a daughter whom she has relinquished to another couple in an open adoption where she has periodic contact with the family:

It hurts a lot more to see Mya. Every time I see her, she has a lot more personality. It's breathtaking. . . . It used to be after I left I would always cry. Sometimes I feel empty when I leave. It's gotten easier though. (Saint Louis 2001, 24)

July 3

We were in Iowa City for the last week or so, bringing Harry home and visiting Audrey and Alan, my sister and brother-in-law. It was very relaxing. We spent a lot of time sitting on their back deck that has an enormous tree that shades it. We would sit out there with our iced tea, taking turns holding Cecilia while the three older children played imaginary creature games among the trees in the backyard or Lego in the playroom. Inevitably the conversation turned to Cecilia's future. We talked about how it would be best for Cecilia to live with her birth sister, as it didn't seem at this point that her mother was making the progress necessary to get her children back. The sister who was older than Cecilia had entered foster care the previous year and therefore the time schedule for planning purposes was farther along. I expressed my hesitancy about this plan, saying that I was concerned because I thought the foster mother who was preadoptive for the sister didn't seem interested in Cecilia. While the foster mother was clearly attached to the sister, whom she had had since birth, she never asked me any questions about Cecilia. I couldn't understand this. I thought that she would favor the sister if she had both girls.

It was hard for me to separate my own feelings for my sisters, whom I love dearly, when thinking about Cecilia living with her sister. ACS has a clear policy of placing children with their siblings if at all possible. Which of course, is mostly a good thing. But what if the siblings have never lived together? What if the adoptive parents can meet the needs of one child but not of two, three, or four children, especially if one or more of the children have special needs? Is it always a good policy to put siblings together, even if it means disrupting bonds that they have formed with other caretakers or foster siblings?

Audrey, who was thinking of having a second child herself, was particularly smitten. We talked about how most of the older cousins were born within a few years of each other and how well they played together. We couldn't resist the mention of a second group (even though we *knew* this baby was not staying).

Now that we have returned home, I have begun waking up in the middle of the night again, in an anxious sweat. I go from being sound asleep to being totally awake in an instant, the house completely quiet. At the moment that I am awake I immediately think of Cecilia and what will happen to her. I remember from some class that I have taken that this type of sleep problem indicates anxiety. Not that I couldn't have figured this out myself—what is surprising to me is the depth and intensity of feelings. I have never been upset to this degree in my life. I feel overwhelmed by what we have done and wonder how it will all turn out. During those moments, I feel that the system is totally fucked up and can never work. I know (intellectually) this baby is not mine, but she doesn't know that I am not her "mother." The days are easier because mostly I think about managing the practical things. I need to provide enough nurturing so that this child can grow up emotionally healthy—I need to be attached (for her) but not *too* attached (for me).

How a Child's Brain Develops
What's Going On: Among the first circuits the brain constructs are those that govern the emotions. Beginning around two months of age, the distress and contentment experienced by newborns start to evolve into more complex feelings: joy and sadness, envy and empathy, pride and shame.

What Parents Can Do: Loving care provides a baby's brain with the right kind of emotional stimulation. Neglecting a baby can produce brain-wave patterns that dampen happy feelings. Abuse can produce heightened anxiety and abnormal stress responses.

Window of Learning: Emotions develop in layers, each more complex than the last. (Nash 1997, 53)

July 12
The summer is going pretty well. It is a huge amount of work with all three kids at home but it is fun too. I really enjoy watching the older kids on a less harried schedule, playing in their pajamas all morning and pulling their rooms apart to play elaborate pretend games. I went to Starbucks this morning with Cecilia, as Peter and Martha were playing with friends. There was a woman there with her mother and a baby that was just a month older than Cecilia. We started talking and she asked me about foster

care. We then talked about her anxiety about returning to work and leaving her daughter with a babysitter. As she was leaving, she turned and said, "God bless you." At first I didn't know what she was talking about and then I realized she was referring to my role as a foster parent. The comment took me off guard because I don't always think of Cecilia as my "foster" daughter. In fact, when she made that comment, I was smugly thinking to myself how well developed Cecilia was—she seemed to be at the same level as this woman's daughter, who was a month older.

Yesterday I went to a training at the agency. Often the best part is listening to the more experienced foster parents talking informally before the training starts. I find it fascinating to hear them speak about their relationships with the children placed in their homes. I am often struck by the way they refer to these kids—often with such pride in the changes the children have made and the way the children still call them as adults to check in (one woman said her foster daughter's children called her "Grandma"). The woman who sat next to me said that she was planning to adopt the first child (now turning three) she had taken in. "I love that little girl," she said with a wistful smile. Another woman who had been a foster parent since the 1970s told me that the hardest thing was seeing the kids leave. She said that when one boy (who in the end did come back to the family and was adopted by them) left, her husband said that he couldn't bear it and to please have the social worker come for the boy while he was at work. She said, "My husband cried, I cried, my mother-in-law, my sister, we all had gotten attached to this kid." But the most rewarding part, she said, is "when they grow up after you raise them and they come back and they thank you for bringing them up and everything. It's a beautiful job."

As Wilkes (1974) has pointed out, the foster family is expected to relate to the child in transition as openly and lovingly as possible. This puts heavy emotional demands on the family members to invest their feelings knowing the relationship must end. Consequently, there may be a natural reluctance to avoid deeper feelings even though emotional distance can be rejecting to all involved. On the other hand, some judge deep emotional involvement as excessive and believe that emotional bonds should be held loose enough to be broken. (Urquhart 1989, 194)

July 14

Yesterday was the six-month permanency planning meeting at the agency. The night before, I woke up feeling anxious and helpless, trying to figure out what was "right" for Cecilia's future. The morning of the meeting, Peter and Martha happily boarded the bus to begin a week of day camp, unaware of the day's importance. Michael was preoccupied with work—something about a lunch seminar for the summer interns. I was left to obsess on my own. I thought about how while we were all affected as a foster family, the details, especially with regard to the agency, were really my "job." I attended all the meetings and would feed the information I gathered and my impressions back to Michael on the telephone during the day and in the evening in person. I was the intermediary between home and the agency. I knew while I was evaluating the agency employees and other extended birth family members who occasionally attended visits, they were also evaluating us as a family, through me and my actions. It was a lot of pressure. I wondered if I was interpreting things accurately and if I had enough information to come to conclusions. I also felt completely exasperated with the system—it seemed ridiculous to ask anyone to take a child on a long-term temporary (isn't this phrase an oxymoron?) basis and treat her like your own but *never* forget that she isn't your own.

I arrived to the meeting a few minutes early and Zuri was sitting in the waiting room by herself. After I signed in, I pushed the stroller over to her and sat next to her. Cecilia looked at her mother and began to cry. I spoke to Cecilia in a reassuring voice and she quieted down. I had brought a bagel with me which I offered to Zuri and she declined. As I ate my snack, Zuri began to play with her daughter and talk to her in a soothing baby-talk voice.

The meeting was interesting but stressful. I got to hear more information about Cecilia's half sisters. They also attended the meeting with their foster mothers. It dawned on me that I didn't even know the other foster parents' names after five months of working with the same family—which I felt was rather pathetic. The part of the meeting that was most painful to me was when the social worker documented with Zuri the obligations that she had not met. While I understood the necessity of the meeting, because I know this mother loves her girls, it was excruciating to witness. I spent a lot of my time watching the girls and their interactions with their mother and their mother's mother, who had also come to the meeting but did not say anything. The older two girls were clearly attached to their mother, grandmother, and foster mother (Simone). They spent their time walking between their mother (at the head of the table) and grandmother and foster mother (seated a few chairs away at the side of the table), alternatively sitting on the laps of these women. Dawn, who is just older than Cecilia, played close to her foster mother, Lorraine, and eventually fell asleep on her lap. Rather than sitting at the large oval wooden table like the rest of us, Lorraine sat back from the table, in a chair against the wall. Cecilia sat on my lap. Simone sat to my left and gave me little parenting tips such as how I should put a bib on Cecilia so that I could wipe her up if she drools. It was annoying, but at the same time I was happy to have the interaction to get to know her better.

The goal for Cecilia was "return to mother" as the agency continued to try and help her birth mother, as they are legally obligated to do for twelve to fifteen months. For the older girls, who had been in care for at least fifteen of the most recent twenty-two months (when the law states that the agency must move to terminate parental rights if the parent has not make progress), it was documented that the foster mothers were preadoptive. After Lorraine was asked whether she was still interested in adopting her foster daughter, she said yes and then turned to the birth mother and said in an apologetic tone, "You know, if things don't work out for you."

I asked about progress in locating Cecilia's birth father—none had been made. I also asked, with my heart thumping, about the time schedule for moving Cecilia with her sister. The other foster mother, Lorraine, said she was still interested in taking Cecilia when space becomes available, after another child in her care returns home to his mother. No one seemed to know exactly when this would happen. I said that I wasn't sure this casual time frame was in Cecilia's best interest—she was growing more and more attached each day (not to mention us to her). I didn't dare say, "She needs a permanent home now." The social worker replied, "If the home becomes available in a month, Cecilia will be moved, but probably not if it is in, say, seven months." What exactly would happen if the time extended to seven months was not addressed. There were so many variables still in play. I didn't reply but felt terrible left hanging in that way and disagreed sharply with what felt like too casual an approach to permanency planning for what increasingly was beginning to feel like my child. I, personally, and we as a family have invested a lot in this child. I have begun to feel proprietary—I feel unsure if I can trust someone else to continue doing a good job raising her. The meeting was strange for me because while I had sat in the social worker's "seat," I now knew what it was like to sit in the other chair. This was one of many cases for the social worker, but this was my life and I loved this child.

Once formed, of course, there is no more powerful emotional glue than an infant's attachment to a favorite caretaker, and yet even this bond, if broken can be reforged with someone else (though there are limits, which vary from individual to individual, to the elasticity of learned trust). But what predisposes an infant to attach to one person rather than another? And why is it that, hands down, the mother so often emerges as the frontrunner for infant affections? It's not *just* a matter of her milk.

It is not preordained that the infant's primary attachment will be to the mother. There are other options. But when you consider that the mother usually has a lower threshold for responding to infant needs, and is the first to respond to a cry of discomfort, with her face, her voice, her breasts, the satisfying sweet milk they spurt in the baby's mouth—-these attributes make the mother the likeliest prospect for her infant to form a primary attachment to. But second-best has proved adequate enough. In fact, when the allo-mother [substitute mother figure] is more committed than the mother, second-best may be superior. (Hrdy 1999, 501)

July 24

Martha came into my bedroom today while I was folding clothes. She plopped herself on the bed and started rolling around. She announced, "I have two mommies."

I said, "Really? And who is the other?"

She replied, "Well, you know that Cecilia and I are sisters and since she has another mom, I must too. But I think that you are a better mommy."

I haven't found much literature on the effects of foster parenting on the birth children but I realize now that it is something that we totally underestimated. I never thought about how attached they would get. Not only do I have to worry about Cecilia but now I also worry about Martha and Peter and how this eventual separation will feel for them. I thought this would be fun for all of us. Now I am feeling guilty, worrying that Martha and Peter may be wounded when Cecilia leaves us. I wonder as their parent if I have been irresponsible bringing another child into our home temporarily.

Michael has been trying to get home in time for dinner on Fridays and we have been trying to stave off our hunger to wait for him. Last Friday, it all managed to happen and we were all sitting around the kitchen table together. Cecilia (now six months old!) wanted to be around everyone else so I was eating with her sitting on my lap. She has recently begun to stick out her tongue, which is quite long, to try and touch her chin—a pretty impressive trick. She started to do this and we all laughed. And she laughed.

We went to a pool party on Sunday out on Long Island. Another guest, a woman I had never met before, told me a story about her family, after meeting Cecilia. She said that when she was very young a female friend of her parents had an affair with a married man and got pregnant. The friend gave birth to a little boy and asked her family to care for him. They called him "Brother." The family pediatrician warned her mother "not to get too attached." However, the inevitable attachment happened and a year later when the married man left his wife and joined his lover, they took their little boy back to raise him themselves, and the woman's family was devastated. Her mother became pregnant immediately and gave birth to a daughter a year later. She said that she feels the loss to this day. This story scared me!

[Concurrent planning] calls for a lot from the foster family. They will know from the start that the child may move back with the birth family or stay to be adopted by them, but they must co-operate with the rehabilitation programme, even though if they are successful it means losing the child. Only pretty special families will be able to resist the temptation to try to sabotage the rehabilitation in order to keep the child for themselves. (Fenton 2001, 17)

July 26

I took Cecilia to our pediatrician for another checkup. Dr. Goodwin weighed and measured her and pronounced her in excellent general health. She reminded me of the real importance of language at this age—"Talk to her all the time." As she sat down to type her notes into the computer, she asked me, "Is it different?"

A simple question, and I knew exactly what she meant. She was asking if it felt different to parent someone else's child compared to a birth child. I said, "You know, it isn't in the day-to-day but then you have the agency, the training, et cetera."

She responded, "A reality check."

"Exactly."

I have begun to think of attachment in a different way. While the child is attaching to you, your attachment to the child is affected by the responsibility you feel toward that child. Much of the essence of parenting has to do with knowing that you are *the* person providing for that child—he or she is relying on you. Having another person or institution with some of the responsibility and control for the child can threaten the sense of responsibility that the parent feels. Unless of course the parent is suspicious of the intentions or doesn't trust the institution (such as in my case—I mean who would? Trusting an institution to care for a child is a crazy idea) and then the abdication of responsibility is mitigated somewhat.

August 12

Martha and Peter went to Albany to visit with their grandparents for the week. Michael and I have been calling them each morning to hear about their adventures. On the second morning,

Peter asked to speak with Cecilia and I held the telephone up to her ear. She looked around with her big eyes and smiled. Later that afternoon, I called Martha to tell her that I found the glasses for her doll that she had been looking for frantically before she left. She said, "Oh. Can I talk to Cecilia?" I said that she was sleeping. Martha replied, "Peter got to." I told her I would call her back when Cecilia woke up.

The visits are improving lately. For three weeks in a row, Cecilia has smiled at her mother instead of crying.

August 30

Last night, I was washing the dishes after dinner, my back facing the kitchen when Martha asked me, "Do you love Cecilia?"

"Yes," I responded slowly, because I could tell by the way she was speaking that it wasn't a simple question.

"Do you love her a lot?"

I began to feel frantic. "Yes," I said.

"Well, then why can't we adopt her?"

I wanted to say, "I know, I know—this is all so difficult isn't it? How is it ever going to work? What will happen?" But instead, I said, "I am not sure adopting her would be the best thing for her." I had already told them that this wasn't really an option anyway.

Then Peter (who was listening to the whole conversation) piped up, "Maybe she could live here and see her sisters and other family on the weekends."

I brought my camera to the visit tonight hoping to get a picture of the whole family. I came in just at the end and when Cecilia saw me, she started reaching for me and crying. I didn't want to snatch her up because this is Zuri's time, but the cries were making everyone stressed and it was painful to ignore her. So I said, "Have you seen Cecilia crawl? Here, let me show you." I took Cecilia from her mother and gave her a little snuggle before I put her on the floor. Her mother and I sat on the floor across from Cecilia and gave her encouragement. Looking very pleased with herself, Cecilia started carefully placing her hands and knees forward. Zuri's sister, who was also at the visit that night, walked by the three of us and said, "I wonder who she will crawl to?" Ouch!

> Attachment behavior is any form of behavior that results in a person attaining or maintaining proximity to some other clearly identified individual who is conceived as better able to cope with the world. It is most obvious whenever the person is frightened, fatigued, or sick, and is assuaged by comforting and caregiving. At other times the behavior is less in evidence. Nevertheless for a person to know that an attachment figure is available and responsible gives him a strong and pervasive feeling of security, and so encourages him to value and continue the relationship. Whilst attachment behavior is at its most obvious in early childhood, it can be observed throughout the life cycle, especially in emergencies. Since it is seen in virtually all human beings (though in varying patterns), it is regarded as an integral part of human nature and one we share (to a varying extent) with members of other species. The biological function attributed to it is that of protection. To remain within easy access of a familiar individual known to be ready and willing to come to our aid in an emergency is clearly a good insurance policy—whatever our age. (Bowlby 1988, 26–27)

Eye of the Storm

AFTER A LONG and busy summer, Martha and Peter returned to school. The first week of September is also Michael's birthday and this year I had planned a dinner party for him. Although I had ordered Indian food and was making only the desserts, it ended up being a lot of work. On the day before the party, Cecilia was quite fussy, and for the first time I felt fed up with her. I was trying to clean up for the party and make dinner for Peter and Martha, who had been at school all day. Michael called from work and I blurted out that if the agency were to come at that moment, I would have given her up. I know that I also felt fed up sometimes with the older two kids when they were young and demanding, but it was never an option to give them back.

The party turned out fine—the weather was nice and we ended

up spending a lot of time on the deck. At my table, one of the guests asked what would happen with Cecilia. I said: "I don't really know. She was supposed to be placed with her half sister but that was months ago. I believe that is still the plan." When people asked about Cecilia's future, I often felt in such a bind. We signed an agreement with the agency and one of the stipulations in the agreement was that we would protect the child's confidentiality. But I found myself often questioning what was confidential. Her past? Her future? And I felt that at some level, privacy must be balanced with honesty. Nothing about Cecilia's history was shameful, and I didn't want to give the impression that it was by keeping secrets. On the other hand, I didn't feel that it was necessary to indulge those just prying for details. A friend who has an adopted daughter said that when people ask her about her adopted child, she inquires if they are interested in adoption or are they just being nosy? Depending on the response, she may or may not share information.

As I was being asked questions, my legs started shaking slightly under the table, a stress reaction that I sometimes have. A friend at the table, David, came to my rescue and said, "I am sure that the baby will end up in a loving home, she is so healthy and good-natured." It is funny how sometimes your body realizes when you are upset before you actually have the thought in your head. When I felt my legs shake, I knew that I was really upset because of the uncertainties that lay ahead regarding what would happen to Cecilia. Even my thought earlier in the day—that I would have given her up at the moment because I was feeling overwhelmed—was really upsetting. When I put Cecilia to bed that night, I paused to look at her for a moment. She seemed so relaxed and happy to be in her bed—so serene—and I felt guilty that I could have even had that thought.

As I struggled to meet the needs of the three children (I had become spoiled in just one week with Michael's help on vacation),

I began to question my commitment to the whole foster care process. How long could I go on with no certainties? I began to note how physically tired I was after carrying Cecilia and pushing the stroller for the day. I also felt that I needed to get out of the house a few days a week, and I wondered if that was influencing my feelings. When I asked Michael's grandmother earlier that summer what it had been like to go back to work after being home for years, she replied, "It was liberating—to get out and not think about the house all day."

As my anxiety grew, I decided that I needed to be more proactive. The first item on my list was Cecilia's birth father. I called the lawyer at Legal Aid at the number I had been given the day after Cecilia arrived, now seven months ago. When I asked her about Cecilia's father, she informed me that it was the agency's obligation to track down the birth father. She said there was really nothing for me to do right now but wait. I was interested in the agency focus on birth mothers, something I had noticed in internships as well. As far as most social service agencies (and maybe most of society) are concerned, mothers are it.

As part of my proactive stance, I bought a book entitled *Children Can't Wait: Reducing Delays for Children in Foster Care.* The book notes that in New York State, if a father is not married to the mother of a child, there are three levels of obligation to the father depending on his level of interaction with the child. At the highest level, where the father has spent time with the child and provided some monetary support, a child cannot be placed for adoption unless the father has surrendered his rights or they have been terminated. At the lowest level, where there is no contact, no support, and no official recognition of the person as the father, there is no obligation to contact the father before the child is placed for adoption. In contrast, six months must pass with no contact from the birth mother before the child is considered abandoned and the child can be freed for adoption. I wondered whether it was reasonable to hold mothers up as more responsible or whether this was a self-fulfilling prophecy. More services are offered to mothers and their parental rights are more carefully guarded, which makes it even more likely that they will end up with the children.

The agency had a name and a nonworking cell-phone number for the alleged father. No one had ever mentioned making other efforts to track him down. I wanted to know if he or his family would be good caretakers for Cecilia—or I wanted to make sure that we would never hear from him. I didn't want him to pop up at the last minute. The second issue was Cecilia's mother. I confirmed that the agency was moving toward a termination of parental rights. I asked on what grounds this was being pursued and the lawyer told me "neglect." I asked why it was not being pursued due to her mental retardation. The lawyer said that the decision was made by the agency and the agency's lawyer. But in her opinion, pursuing a termination of parental rights due to mental retardation was a "sadder" course to take. She also said it could be more complicated to document. I didn't know anything about the legal process but I found it interesting that the birth mother's feelings (or maybe it was the lawyer's feelings) were being taken into account in this respect—first, because this process was supposed to be about Cecilia and her best interests, not her mother's; and second, because rather than acknowledging the mother's limitations, the court has made demands on her that she most likely won't be able to meet and then it will find her neglectful. And this was less sad?

In September, I went to my book group for the first time since Cecilia arrived. It was nice to get out in the evening, but once again, I felt a little overwhelmed by the curiosity about Cecilia's future. As I was beginning to explain for the third time to a woman I really don't know well what might happen to Cecilia, I said, "I don't feel that comfortable talking about this because I really have no idea what is going to happen." It was liberating to say it and she backed off immediately.

One Thursday morning in mid-September, Summer (the new social worker, as the previous one had moved to Boston) called me to see why I hadn't attended the previous night's visit. I reminded her that I had taken Cecilia to the agency Medical Department for an appointment that same day and therefore wasn't obligated to go to the visit that night. I had tried to contact Summer to remind her before the visit but was unable to reach her. We started talking (Summer seemed much more approachable to me than Miriam, the previous social worker) and Summer mentioned that she was getting a lot of pressure from Administration for Children's Services to place Cecilia in the foster home where her older half sister, Dawn, lives. Summer told me that the other child in that home was approved to go home the day his mother found housing. The social worker reminded me that ACS tries to adhere to a policy of keeping siblings together. I said that while I understood the value of the policy, we should be clear that this baby had never lived with her siblings; in fact, from her perspective, Peter and Martha were her siblings. I asked whether Dawn's foster mother, Lorraine, would be interested in adopting Cecilia, should she be freed for adoption. I told Summer that I had been reading some articles that noted the dangers of moving children through too many placements. It isn't very difficult to understand that moving children from home to home is damaging for them. And perhaps because of the cumulative effect of this damage, which often manifests itself in the form of very difficult behavior, the more often a child moves, the more likely she is to move again. I said to Summer: "I know you are still working with the birth mother but since there is the possibility that she won't get her act together and that her parental rights would be terminated, Cecilia should go to a home where there is the option of adoption." Summer said she would follow up with Lorraine.

The social worker was good-natured about all my questions

and comments. Her openness allowed me to ask about something else that I had been worried about—the services that the birth mother was receiving. While I had resigned myself to focus on what I could do for the baby and leave her mother to the agency social workers, I reached a point where I felt I had to choose a path and advocate in that direction. Was this baby going back to her birth mother or not? One of the things I was concerned about was whether Zuri was getting appropriate services. I worried about this for two reasons. One was that it seemed immoral not to give this woman every possible option to have her child back. I asked my mother, who had made her career as a social worker with the New York State Office of Mental Retardation and Developmental Disabilities, how Cecilia's mother could be helped. She said that it was difficult and that often parents with mental retardation would benefit from supervised housing with their children. She also said that there were very few placements like this and that the birth mother would have to want to live there. In her experience, people who haven't grown up with a lot of structure and supervision don't willingly choose this option.

My second reason for worry was that even if the agency made the determination that this mother couldn't be an adequate parent, if they didn't do their job and offer appropriate services (I believe that the judge had ordered parenting classes and some type of day-treatment program for drug use), the court would not terminate the parental rights and Cecilia would stay in care longer. I was reassured by Summer's compassionate tone toward Zuri and what seemed a thorough approach to providing appropriate services at a good agency (although I don't think Zuri was attending the classes). At one point, I asked Cecilia's mother: "I know it is none of my business, but do you feel that the agency is helping you? Are they doing what they need to, to help you?" Zuri replied that they were, but it is quite likely that she didn't trust me enough to be honest.

My conversation with Summer and its serious tone took me

by surprise and made me wrestle (once again) with our role in Cecilia's future. It also made me feel tired with the whole discussion and made me wish for some resolution.

At the same time I was thinking about Cecilia's future, I was making plans at home for her. Cecilia was now an adorable eight-month-old. She could play quite happily and independently for short periods. She would sit on the floor, picking up toys and chewing on them, scooting over to investigate others. I decided to investigate a playgroup, thinking that she would enjoy seeing the other babies. The social worker at the Early Intervention program suggested organizing a group of parents from my community with similar age babies. The first meeting was held at a woman named Michelle's house and she was quite welcoming. She had even made banana bread and coffee for us. It was fun to meet the other mothers and babies but I felt a little out of place. Cecilia was creeping over to the other babies and grabbing at them so I had to restrain her a lot. While it was interesting to meet these women, they shared a connection through their children, all of whom were their birth children and had serious medical problems. The mothers could share their worries and their anxieties about their children's physical and intellectual development. I had a completely different set of worries, and while the women were sweet and sympathetic, I really didn't feel that I was a good fit for the group.

One morning about this time, I met a woman while in line for a cup of coffee at Starbucks who said that her husband had been in foster care (and moved several times before finding the right place), that they have one son, and that they were considering becoming foster parents. I encouraged her and gave her my number if she wanted to talk more about it. I said that I thought the most important thing was to be clear on what you wanted out of it so you could have the right mindset. I then went to my friend Karen's and as I was telling her about the conversation, it occurred to me that while I had thought we were entirely clear that we were only going to be foster parents, *I* had changed my mind. I was attached and I had begun to think about adoption, although I felt selfish doing so because I thought Cecilia's life would be less difficult with a black family.

It might have been this change of heart that made the visit with the birth family so miserable one night at the end of September. I had by now developed ways in which I fed and interacted with Cecilia that she was comfortable with. And of course, the birth mother had her own style of parenting. I felt as if maybe I was giving up on any hope of reunification.

During the visit, I met my sister Natalie to go shopping. While I used to really enjoy shopping, especially the hunt for a great deal, I rarely had time anymore. However, that evening it was a relief to abandon myself to such a mindless activity and I bought two discounted sweaters. As we stood in line to pay for our items, I told Natalie how stressful it was for me to leave Cecilia at the agency now. The people were unfamiliar to her and the environment was chaotic. Cecilia seemed so unhappy there and it pained me to feel that I was abandoning her.

After shopping, I picked Cecilia up at the agency and took her home on the subway. I had her in the backpack, and as I descended the stairs, she bounced in the backpack in a joyful manner. On the train, she captivated several nearby passengers with her baby flirting. When I got home, I felt completely exhausted. That night after going to sleep, I had stress dreams. In one, buildings were collapsing nearby and I was desperately trying to figure out how to help the people inside.

Michael and I began to have discussions about the possibility of adopting, but it was difficult to discuss the topic in depth because it was all theoretical. We had become foster parents knowing that we were happy with two children. Otherwise, we would have looked for an adoptive placement straightaway. And we probably wouldn't have considered foster care because we hadn't understood initially how many foster care placements turn into adoptive placements. In any event, Cecilia wasn't available for adoption and the system had made it clear that we weren't her parents. We had tried to be true to this arrangement. We did talk about how things were turning out differently than we expected. We had hoped to help reunite a family and it was beginning to look increasingly unlikely that that would happen. One night as Peter was playing with Cecilia, he said he was really happy that she had come to live with us because he had really enjoyed the experience. When I told Michael about this, we talked about how if we ever did take in another child (which had been our plan), Peter and Martha would probably never bond in the same way—saying that they preferred Cecilia. At about the same time, Martha also expressed her enjoyment with having Cecilia live with us. In fact, after a fight during which Peter accidentally got kneed in the head while he and Martha were competing for Cecilia's attention, Martha said to me, "It's too bad we don't have a human copier and then we could each have a Cecilia to play with"—although Martha also said that she had not considered the difficult parts of having a baby, such as when the baby pulls her hair or yells in the car.

At the end of September, Summer called and told me that she had asked Lorraine about her intentions with regard to Cecilia and Lorraine said that she was planning to move to Seattle as soon as Dawn's adoption goes through. I was shocked at this news but also surprised at my happy feelings when I quickly realized that this would give us a better place in the lineup. I told Summer again that we weren't in any hurry, but she said that ACS was on her back—she would meet with her supervisor and begin working on permanency plans for Cecilia. It seemed increasingly unlikely that the birth mother would be able to plan appropriately for Cecilia's return, so an alternate permanency plan was needed. It was funny that I said we weren't in any hurry because I felt an unbearable pressure to resolve the situation. At the same time, I was so uncertain what the right resolution was that I wanted to stall for more time.

On the last day of September, Martha, Peter, Cecilia, and I went out for dinner. First, we stopped at a children's clothes store. I had to buy shoes for Cecilia because it was getting cold and she kept pulling her socks off. We chose some cute little red leather boots. At the Japanese restaurant on the same block, we talked about how we had come to that same restaurant the night Cecilia arrived almost a year earlier. This prompted Peter and Martha to talk about their feelings. Peter brought up that he really wanted to adopt Cecilia and Martha said she did as well. I said that we needed to include Daddy in this discussion. Martha said, " Yeah, we need a family meeting." I reminded them that Cecilia was supposed to be placed with her birth sister. I mentioned that I thought it might be difficult for Cecilia to be the only black person in our family and Peter fantasized that we could paint ourselves black and Martha responded, "Or we could paint Cecilia white."

October brought a series of complicated discussions between Michael and me as we tried to grapple with Cecilia's future. Michael would say how he worried about his capacity to parent a third child forever, although he had enjoyed parenting Cecilia thus far. He said that while he had considered the idea of adoption, he felt conflicted changing direction from our original role as foster parents. The discussion was typical for us. While I tend to think things through quickly, Michael protects his emotions more and makes more careful decisions. Michael also said that he considered whether he should go through with it for my, Peter, and Martha's sake but that he felt anxious about committing until his own feelings were sorted out.

While I had some hesitation, I mostly felt a reawakening of my maternal feelings and the joy of having a young developing person (some of the feelings I had forgotten about somewhat from when Peter and Martha were little). We both felt that life would be easier for Cecilia if her adoptive parents were black. The color of her parents would affect her entire life and it was difficult thinking about such an important decision when no one could know how she would feel about the decision as an adult. Making a decision of this magnitude for her weighed heavily on us. This was a very difficult time, trying to make choices about decisions that were abstract. Probably the only good thing was that we both felt committed to staying on the same track. We had gone into this together and there was little point in letting it drive us apart.

One Monday morning after a weekend of difficult discussions, I accompanied Martha's class on an apple-picking trip. My seatmate on the trip was the grandmother of one of Martha's classmates. She asked how many children I had, which led to a discussion of Cecilia. She asked if we planned to adopt her. I felt my eyes well with tears. I explained that we had little choice in the matter but if asked I would like to consider it, although my husband felt anxious about the whole idea. She responded, "Don't mess up your marriage." Around this same time, I had a similar conversation at the park with a black woman who was pushing the child she babysat for in the swing next to the one I was pushing Cecilia in. After I answered her questions, she said, "You should think about adopting her."

I said, "Don't you think it would be difficult for her to be the only black person in a white family?"

She paused. "Yes, it would be." She seemed to consider my question with care, and I appreciated that. "But love is important too."

Almost simultaneously, I had conversations with two friends in our neighborhood who both mentioned that they knew a black couple who were interested in adopting. I suggested to both that they have their friends call me. However, it was hard to imagine how the whole process would work out.

On one overwhelming day at the beginning of October, I talked to both couples who were interested in Cecilia. First, Amy called. She was pleasant but I felt a bit uptight (although considering the nature of our conversation, perhaps this was understandable). She seemed very particular about details about Cecilia. For example, I mentioned that Cecilia was chunky (which I meant in a cute baby sort of way) and she later asked me if any of Cecilia's birth sisters were overweight. That was a bit difficult for me. It was impossible for me to talk in a detached and objective manner about this child I had raised. Amy also said that they were completely against any contact with the birth family, and that bothered me. She mentioned that they were in a pool of thirty-five couples at a Manhattan-based private adoption agency waiting for infants; none were currently available and if they were, the birth mothers would have the option of picking the adoptive parents. We ended the conversation saying that we would be back in touch after I spoke with the foster care agency. After speaking with Amy, I called Summer and explained the situation. Summer felt it was a long shot but a possibility. She explained the lineup to me—first would be the birth mother, second would be the home where Cecilia's half sister lived, third would be us, and this couple would be fourth. Summer said she would check into it.

At 5:45 the same day, the second couple, Peter and Cynthia, called just as I was making banana pancakes for dinner. They were both on the line and I thought that was great. Something about them struck me as very warm—for example, when I mentioned that another couple had just called, Peter, said, "Oh, really" in a disappointed way. I gave a quick description of Cecilia and they told me a little about themselves. Peter said: "We are both African

American. I am dark and my wife is light and so the baby could identify with us no matter the tone of her color. That is an important issue in our culture." When he said this to me, something clicked and I knew I was doing the right thing. They told me about their house, which had a bedroom waiting and a yard. They said they wouldn't want Cecilia to be an only child and would work on having more children. They asked if they could be approved as foster parents in less than six months. I mentioned keeping in touch with her sisters and they seemed open to considering the idea. I said I would speak with Summer on Tuesday and get back to them. I felt sort of excited after speaking with them; they seemed so kind and warm. However, I was exhausted for the rest of the evening and after Martha woke me at five the next morning, I lay in bed in shock thinking about what I was doing.

Over the next few days, I mulled over how this would all work. I wondered whether, if one of these families worked out as adoptive parents, they would consider maintaining contact with us as well. As I toyed with the idea of Cecilia leaving, I started daydreaming about our continued relationship. It was no longer bearable for her to just move on; we had decided that wherever she went, we must keep in contact. I ran through different scenarios—attending her birthday parties, babysitting once a week, taking her for the weekend. I thought about having a going-away party that would include her new family and us. I decided that if the transition did become a probability, we should begin visits as soon as possible and extend them over several months, making the transition as painless as possible for Cecilia.

At the next visit a few days later, Summer said that Cynthia had repeatedly tried to contact her that day (as I had) and that they had finally spoken. Summer referred Cynthia to Homefinders, the agency division for adoptive families for children in foster care, to find out the requirements for preadoptive parents. However, Summer said that there had been a new development: Lorraine, the foster mother of Cecilia's half sister, had changed her mind and was now interested in taking Cecilia. The other child in Lorraine's home would be leaving in six to eight weeks, as Summer had received a letter from the housing authority saying that housing would finally become available for that child's mother. Although Lorraine was African American and the half sisters living together could be a real positive, I mentioned that in the visits, Lorraine had seemed completely uninterested in Cecilia, and that concerned me. Summer said that during the next six to eight weeks, Lorraine would spend half an hour or so at each visit every other week "trying to develop a bond" with Cecilia. I was shocked by Lorraine's change of heart and mistrustful of her intentions. I thought the idea of bonding for a half-hour every other week was preposterous. During the visit, I went outside in complete distress and called Michael. Michael was also distressed, and we discussed how best to react to this news.

I came back to the agency fifteen minutes before the visit was due to end to talk to Lorraine but she had already left, so Summer suggested that we talk in two weeks, at the next visit. I said rather than wait, Summer should feel free to give Lorraine my phone number. As I went home on the subway, I felt completely in over my head. As usual, Cecilia was extremely cheerful on the way home and bounced in the backpack with pleasure. She worked hard to get the attention of two older Asian women next to us, smiling with her whole face (she has very expressive eyes), and snorted, coughed and grabbed at the sleeve of the woman closest to us until the two stopped talking and started paying attention, tickling Cecilia and laughing with her until our stop.

In the next week, I had two awkward calls with the African American families I had met through my friends. They seemed discouraged and uninterested in getting involved in our tangled mess. I wanted to say: "Have courage and strength. Stick it out." But they just wanted a baby. Neither couple was interested in becoming part of this multifaceted saga with several possible endings. I knew that without a lot of conviction to follow through over the next few months, they would never make it through the uncertainty, so I didn't bother encouraging them any further and wished them well.

As awful and stressful as this time was, I was beginning to see that the agency did pay some attention to our opinions now that some planning was under way and we were clear that we cared. When a mother at the playground asked me about foster care, I surprised myself by responding positively in the midst of our confusion. I had just had a conversation with Simone, the foster mother of two of the older half siblings, that week. She told me that she and her husband planned to adopt Brittney and MaryKate. She seemed a little hesitant but said her husband really wanted to. While Simone spent some time criticizing the girls, including lamenting the fact that she couldn't "whoop their butts," she also seemed upset that she had to leave them with strangers (certified by the agency) that weekend while she went to a wedding in Maryland. She had wanted to leave them with friends she trusted from her church. It was a relief to see that these girls were on their way to a permanent home, however awkwardly and slowly the process was working.

In October, my mother and sister Audrey and her family came to visit. I was excited for them to see Cecilia, who had changed so much. In fact, she was now a bit of a challenge as she was crawling everywhere and trying to get into everything. Cecilia could also now understand the words "clap," "kiss," and "no" and respond appropriately. Cecilia got all excited when she saw my nephew, Andrew—she clearly remembered him from the summer. My other sister, Natalie, said that Andrew talked a lot about Cecilia. Harry, another nephew, seemed happy and interested to see Cecilia again as well. I realized that the developing bonds were not limited to our immediate family but included the entire extended family, an understanding that made my desire to resolve the situation even stronger.

The more time that passed, the more sensitive I felt about questions from strangers about Cecilia's future, despite my incessant desire to discuss the situation with family and close friends. Strangers' questions hit a raw nerve. When I went to the WIC office (which I found alternately interesting and trying), the nutritionist who had given the little lecture on food content interviewed me on Cecilia's eating habits. She then asked point-blank if we were going to adopt Cecilia and whether I had other children. Because I found her questions so rude and invasive, that was the last time I went to the WIC office.

In another instance, I took the kids out to buy sneakers. Afterward, we stopped at the news shop to buy a candy treat. The man behind the counter, who looked and sounded Indian, asked in broken English where I got Cecilia and then came over to talk to her. He spoke to the woman behind the counter in their native language, although she seemed much less interested. The man was captivated and kept asking the woman to take a closer look at Cecilia. After we escaped out the door, I commented to Martha and Peter that these constant public interventions can be annoying, and they agreed. It occurred to me that same-race care or adoption, in some situations, would not only make things easier for the child in foster care but for the biological children as well.

Sometimes I overheard Peter cooing to Cecilia, "I love you. I love you." Hearing him made me joyful and frightened at the same time. It is satisfying to see your children grow to love each other but in this situation, I worried how they would be hurt when eventually separated. Martha was also bonding more deeply with Cecilia, and she in some ways had it even harder because she was coming to accept that she was giving up her position as the youngest and the only girl. Sometimes she expressed jealousy. Although she could read extremely well, Martha complained that

I didn't read to her because Cecilia took up too much of my time. She also said Cecilia was very noisy, and she once asked whom I loved more. Martha was growing to accept Cecilia as a real member of our family. At the same time, Martha genuinely seemed to care for Cecilia, whom she once described as "hungry, lovable, and loud." She played with her constantly and always included her in her thoughts. For example, when buying sneakers at the shoe store, Martha pointed out several pairs of sneakers and sandals that she thought we should get for Cecilia when she got bigger. I felt that if Cecilia were a permanent member of our family, I could have dealt with the jealousy more easily. Although I loved my younger sister, Natalie, who was very cute and got lots of attention when we were growing up, I was jealous at times of her. I found Martha's feelings completely normal, but the abnormal situation made me feel guilty all around.

I began to grow fed up with the whole foster care experience (although not with Cecilia) and felt convinced that I did not have the energy to do it again with another child. While I would have loved to be a foster parent to many more children, I realized that I didn't have the strength. Either I wasn't the right type of person, the system was too difficult, or both. I felt we had done a good job and I was proud of that, but I couldn't develop another relationship that involved so much uncertainty again.

Lorraine didn't call me during the two-week period between visits and I was apprehensive about what would happen at the next visit. I ran into Lorraine by the elevator as I arrived and said that I wanted to talk to her. We agreed to meet by the visit room.

I can't remember how I addressed the issue, but Lorraine immediately told me that, in fact, she wasn't interested in taking Cecilia, as she was so busy with Dawn and her needs. Lorraine said that she had taken Dawn because she felt that Dawn had no one and because her older daughters were very attached to Dawn. Lorraine clearly loved Dawn as well. For some time, I had noticed

the attention she gave to Dawn and the bond between them. She
said that the social worker told her that Cecilia was being moved
to another couple but not that I had a personal connection with
them. She said she had felt pressured to take Cecilia and it was
implied that Dawn's adoption would be held up if she didn't comply. I assured her that I would be responsible for Cecilia's well-
being and that I would not let her be dumped somewhere. I felt
very upset that Lorraine felt pressured to take Cecilia (especially
because I worried what implications this would have for Cecilia
and whether Dawn would be favored).

Lorraine also said that the social worker told her she should
bond with Cecilia in fifteen minutes or so every two weeks and
that she had told her daughter this was ridiculous. I told her I
had said the same thing to my family. Lorraine said she felt that
the agency was pushing for the sisters to live together just so the
agency could look better to ACS. She told me she still intended to
move to Seattle as soon as Dawn's adoption went through (since
Dawn was older, she already had a court case pending to terminate the birth mother's rights). Lorraine said she was also upset
that the other child in her home had not been reunited with his
mother yet, and she felt that the agency had not been entirely
straight with her about the housing situation. She told me she
had dealt with six social workers since Dawn came to live with
her almost two years ago and advised me that as soon as the social
worker starts taking time off, you know she is going to leave. I was
aghast and did not want to believe her, but it was true that the
previous social worker had left shortly after taking her vacation (to
interview for a new job in another city). I felt really relieved after
our discussion that Lorraine had been honest with me about her
intentions toward Cecilia. I was also a little sorry that she wasn't
in a position to take both girls, because she did seem competent
and loving. We exchanged telephone numbers so that we could
keep in touch.

It was now the beginning of November and I was absolutely

consumed with thoughts of Cecilia's future. I spoke about this uncertainty with Michael, my sisters, my mother, and my friend Karen. It was all I thought about, and it was torture. On the first Friday in November, I went to Albany to visit my mother and my sister Lynn. I was looking forward to my first night away from the children since Cecilia had arrived and hoped the distance might clear my head and do me some good. On the train ride there, just for fun I used my new cell phone to call home to see how things were going. No one answered and I began to worry. The babysitter should have been home with the children. I called again and again and finally got through around seven o'clock, just as we sat down and ordered our dinner at the restaurant. Michael said I had forgotten to give the babysitter the keys to the house and so the children had been at the babysitter's apartment until he got home from work. He asked me to hold on a minute, and I could hear him shooing Martha and Peter upstairs out of hearing distance. He got back on the telephone and told me that Summer had left a message that Cecilia was going to be removed from our home next week to another home with Dawn. I was stunned. Noticing my tone or my expression or both, my mother, stepfather, and Lynn stopped talking. With their eyes riveted on my face, they asked: "What's wrong? Sarah, what's wrong?"

I felt devastated and bewildered. I explained to my family what Michael told me. None of us knew what to say. The chicken and rice that I had ordered before I placed the phone call was put on the table in front of me. I had to force myself to eat a few bites. My mother and sister suggested that I could go home the next morning, but I decided it would be pointless since we wouldn't know anything new until Monday.

I hardly slept that night. I was so distressed that I was grateful I had come to visit supportive family members and didn't have to put on an act in front of friends who might not understand how I felt. I spoke with Michael several times on Saturday. He said he had played Summer's message over and over, trying to understand exactly what it said. I felt a little better when he told me that the message didn't seem to say that Cecilia would be moved to Lorraine's house. He said it all seemed a bit vague. I tried calling Lorraine several times on Friday and Saturday and once on Sunday and then decided that I really didn't know if she knew what was going on and that I didn't want to be the one to tell her. On Saturday we went shopping and stopped at a bookstore, where I bought *Adopting in America: How to Adopt within One Year*. I honestly don't know what I was thinking but I felt compelled to buy it.

I came home Saturday night and Michael and I spoke that night and the next day. We both felt stressed, upset, and pressured. We talked about all the options we could think of—sometimes arguing but mostly trying to work together so we wouldn't damage our own relationship. Michael especially felt manipulated by the agency. He could not understand how a child who was placed with us in February and was supposed to be moving to be with her sister in June was in November suddenly moving somewhere else. He was right that it was ridiculous but having more experience with the system, I knew that what was happening was not intentional or especially uncommon. For us, it was personal and painful but we were just one couple in an overwhelmed and underfunded system.

I called the agency first thing on Monday morning, but I had to wait an excruciating half hour before I spoke to Summer's supervisor, JoAnn (Summer was in court, I think). She apologized and said that Summer wasn't thinking clearly when she left a message on our answering machine on a Friday afternoon with that type of information. She said that something had happened and that Dawn was going to be removed from Lorraine's home—What was going on?—although Lorraine didn't know it yet, as she had been in Seattle. I said I was confused and concerned. JoAnn told me there was no rush in Cecilia's case, but Dawn was going to be moved to a new foster home that week—unless, of course, we would take Dawn also. I said that was a firm no. Dawn, exactly one year older than Cecilia, was almost two. Unlike the previous year when I was only imagining what it would be like to be a foster parent, I was now firmly rooted in reality. While it was a tiny bit tempting to imagine taking Dawn, I knew that I was just managing with three children. JoAnn said that the new foster parent was experienced and was interested in adopting both girls. I asked what race the foster mother was and she replied, "Black." I said that I wanted what was best for Cecilia and it was hard to tell what that was at this point. JoAnn referred to the bond between the girls.

I said, "They have never lived together."

"But they see each other in the visits," JoAnn said.

"Cecilia cries through them until I get there," I told her.

We agreed that we needed to sit down together and sort the situation out. We set up a meeting for November 16, the following week. I felt very relieved and called Michael and my mother, who also sounded relieved (and somewhat disgusted by the disorganized and inappropriate way things were being handled). Michael was also upset about Dawn being removed from Lorraine's home and said that he thought Lorraine should hire a lawyer. He even suggested that maybe his law firm could take on the case pro bono.

Two days later, I went to the Wednesday night family visit with interest. I met the new foster parent for Dawn, her twenty-second child from foster care, whom she was hoping to adopt. The new foster mother told me that she had been adopted herself. In terms of color, she was no browner than I am, so I was uncertain what the social worker was talking about. She was nice enough but when I met this woman and her daughter, I thought that I would never let Cecilia live with them. She was different from my fantasy of a warm childless adoptive person or couple. She wasn't of the same race as Cecilia (clearly, JoAnn had gotten confused about this). She was a single mother whose three teenaged daughters helped her care daily for children she took in. (This was a contrast to Lorraine, who bragged of the achievements of her twin twenty-year-old daughters; Lorraine was quite proud that one was in the navy.) If I had been a caseworker, this would have been a great placement for a child because the woman was warm and experienced, but it was not what I wanted for Cecilia. The reality of meeting a complete stranger and considering placing someone I cared about in her home was startling. No way.

I asked the new foster mother how Dawn was adjusting. She said that Dawn was doing pretty well, that she wasn't eating too much, but that she was working on it and had given Dawn a special spoon and plate as encouragement. A few weeks later, I saw Dawn at a visit. I watched her climb up on the social worker's lap and rip the social worker's glasses off. The social worker and I were shocked by how aggressive Dawn was. And then it occurred to me that this poor baby, who had suddenly been removed from the only home she knew and would never have contact with her previous foster mother again, upon coming to the agency, a familiar place, might have felt enraged.

When the social worker wasn't around, Simone, the foster mother of the older half siblings, asked me what was happening. I told her what I knew about Dawn's removal and gave her Lorraine's phone number. I called Lorraine after the visit and she seemed in shock and in pain. Her version of events (which I had no reason not to believe) was that she had gotten upset at the agency for their lack of effort and attention and had hired a lawyer. The lawyer recommended that Lorraine sue the agency. Lorraine said that she threatened to do so in a fight with the supervising social worker. She said the agency then removed the children for her "noncompliance" (illegally, I thought). She was working with her lawyer but felt completely demoralized. I was outraged and disgusted but nervous about compromising our own situation by getting involved. Michael found the whole thing particularly upsetting, and the situation fueled his distrust of the agency.

However, Michael and I began considering adoption more seriously, although the conversations in which we spoke about specifics such as whether we would change Cecilia's name and where her permanent bedroom might be seemed futile. These conversations were always abstract and fanciful because we had no idea what would happen. Foster parents are given priority as preadoptive resources in New York State only after they have had a child for one year. And anyway, the agency had made it clear that the plan was to put Cecilia with her sister. Regardless, I began reading everything I could find on transracial adoption. In some ways, it was just an exercise to pass the time until we met with the agency and worked out a permanent plan.

During that week, I also emptied out half the furniture from my small office. Cecilia had been sharing a bedroom temporarily with Martha, but it didn't work out too well; because of the six-year age difference, they had very different sleeping schedules. So in the half of the office that was empty, I placed Cecilia's crib and changing table. Martha seemed very happy to have her own space back. Cecilia did fine with the move. I kept imagining what a cute little nursery the room would make. The half-moved state of affairs seemed to be a metaphor for the precariousness of Cecilia's situation.

In the meantime, I spoke to Lorraine a few times. She said that she missed Dawn so much that she was having trouble eating and sleeping. But when I encouraged her to follow through on her plan to stand up for herself and Dawn, she said she was having a health problem for which she needed surgery and she needed to address that first. I couldn't understand her delay because I knew to retain any rights she needed to act now. Something told me that maybe there was more to this story. I decided not to press it but told her to call me if she needed help.

It was now mid-November and Michael and I spent a week alternatively arguing and agreeing about Cecilia's situation—it was hard to sum up any final discussion because the topic was so difficult. Michael felt manipulated by the system and the agency because he believed they hadn't done an adequate job of planning for Cecilia. I felt that I had gone beyond that. I had been more involved in the day-to-day process and as a social worker, I knew things didn't always work the way they should. Michael was right about the system, but I pointed out to him that although we were all suffering, this wasn't personal or intentional on the agency's part. As the meeting with JoAnn and Summer at the agency approached, we wrote a list of items we wanted to discuss. Michael and I were nervous but relieved that progress was being made toward a permanent plan.

The meeting took place at 9:30 on a Thursday morning in JoAnn's small, cramped office. We had Cecilia with us and she spent a lot of time trying to crawl under chairs to examine dust in the far corners. After the initial introductions and pleasantries, Summer and JoAnn started right in: "We have decided it is time to move forward with a permanency plan for Cecilia, as she has been in care for almost a year. As you know, we have petitioned the courts to terminate the parental rights for her older siblings. We would like you to be the preadoptive parents for Cecilia. She could be moved to the new foster home where her sister is now living and that foster mother is willing to be preadoptive for both of them. However, Cecilia is obviously very bonded to your family and is thriving. We feel that it is in her best interest to remain with you. If you would like to move her, we will do so in a gradual time frame that feels comfortable for you. If you feel that you would like to be preadoptive, we will speak to ACS and try and convince them that it is in her best interest to stay with you and not move in with her sister." The agency makes a recommendation but ACS as the actual guardian also has a say—the final decision is made by the judge. "However, if they disagree, we will support you and are prepared to do so in court, if necessary. How long do you think you need to make this decision?"

I felt choked with emotion and tears came to my eyes. Michael said, "How about after the holidays?"

This was more than six weeks away. I gasped, "I can't stand it. How about by Monday?"

Michael agreed. His instinctive reaction had been to "play for time," to allow us to discuss things outside the presence of two strangers, particularly given his distrust of the foster care bureaucracy that had so frequently seemed to make rash, sometimes irrational, decisions. In an instant, he looked beyond this issue and made the decision that seemed right in his heart.

We then talked about our concerns about how Cecilia would be affected growing up in a white family. We spoke about the other foster family. The social worker told me that they had some African American relatives, but I said that I had met the family and they appeared white. Summer and JoAnn assured us that our multiracial neighborhood would make it easier for Cecilia.

Before we left, Michael and I asked what had happened with Lorraine. We said that her situation with Dawn had been very confusing and upsetting for us. JoAnn said: "I know. I wish I could tell you what happened but it is confidential. I can only say that it is something personal to Lorraine and we tried for a long time to work it out. When she broke our last agreement, we felt that we had no choice but to move the children. And in fact, she has signed the paperwork, relinquishing any interest in the situation." We understood that it was appropriate to guard Lorraine's privacy but it was hard to comprehend what had happened. The thing that made no sense to us was if the agency thought this woman was having problems, why did they pursue placing Cecilia with her? We felt especially grateful that this had never come to pass—if it had, Cecilia would now be moving with Dawn to her *fourth* home in her first year of life.

The weekend was a blur. Can we do this? Will she resent us some day? We can only do the best we can and hope that she has a happy life. Is this the right decision for Cecilia or are we letting our feelings get in the way of what is right for her?

We realized that if we went forward, we would probably not be foster parents again, a role we had enjoyed. We had looked forward to meeting more children and their families.

We called our close family members, whose responses were honest and supportive:

"If you love her, you should do it."

"You should consider that you will sacrifice your privacy and hers as a multiracial family."

"I thought you had always intended to adopt."

"I probably wouldn't have become a foster parent in the first place, but if I had and I could afford it, I wouldn't give her up."

"She is a human being like any other and deserves a loving home. You should keep her."

"You might not be so lucky next time—such a lovely, bright baby."

"Race won't be an issue—class transcends race in America."

By the end of the weekend, we realized that regardless of whose interests we had at heart, Cecilia's or ours, we couldn't face the prospect of having her move. We were no longer the same people we had been before she arrived. We felt that now, at ten months of age, Cecilia too had been imprinted by us and that she needed us. I called Summer on Monday morning, November 20, and said we had decided to become preadoptive parents.

After the decision was made, we were flooded with relief. Michael and I told Peter and Martha, who were joyful. They wanted to share the news with their friends. We moved the desk and the computer from the office to the family room. We took the calendar and photos off the walls and in their place, we hung children's pictures and an alphabet chart. We put a wicker rocking chair and a small bookcase for children's books and toys in the room. The office was transformed into a little nursery.

When I reflect upon the almost ten months between February 28 and the middle of November, it is difficult to believe what we went through. We had to have a certain elasticity of emotion and attachment to make it through this period. Sometimes we were stretched almost to the point of breaking, but gradually the cord that bound us to Cecilia became more durable, enabling us to hold on to her.

Sometimes I wonder what happened to the other children who were referred to us. I once said to Karen that we were so lucky that it was Cecilia who was placed with us. She said she thought that we would have done the same for any child placed with us. I was taken aback at first because each of our children seem so special to us. But it may be true that we would have worked to integrate whomever fate placed with us in the middle of the night into our family.

7

Transition

MICHAEL AND I were euphoric for several weeks after our decision to adopt Cecilia. It was exciting to think about her being a permanent member of our family and emotionally we charged ahead, ignoring the fact that we were not yet her legal parents and would not be for some time. I day-dreamed about the day the adoption would go through and the party we wanted to have to celebrate. Michael joked that I had it organized down to the dresses the girls would wear. When I told Sheryl, a friend and the babysitter of a friend's child, that we were now preadoptive she cried and then went home and called our friend at work and cried again. We got lots of congratulations and hugs and a few surprised looks from people who thought we were preadoptive already.

After some discussion, we decided that we wanted to change

Cecilia's name to one that wasn't shared with any of our pets and that we felt especially connected to. It was a hard decision to make before the parental rights were even terminated. I was relieved when my mother, often my moral compass, said that she thought that it was our right, considering that we had committed to raising Cecilia.

We took the train up to Montreal for Thanksgiving with my mother and stepfather and on the sixteen-hour roundtrip we spent hours looking through baby name books and making a "top choices" list. I liked "Katherine" but it sounded too Christian for Michael and we already had a cousin with that name. Eventually, we agreed on "Ella," with two middle names. We chose "Lynn" for my sister Lynn and we chose "Cecilia" for Cecilia's birth family. For several months I worried that "Ella" wouldn't be an appropriate name in the black culture—would it sound too white, the way "Katherine" sounded too Christian to Michael? I was relieved when a black woman with whom I had been able to have an honest discussion about black/white relations said, "What a pretty name!" I was even more excited a few years later when I went to a show at the Whitney Museum of quilts made by an isolated group of African American women in Gee's Bend, Louisiana, and one of the artist's names was Ella Mae. Sewing quilts is one of my favorite pastimes and the show was a particularly good one.

We sent out our Christmas letter introducing Cecilia as Ella and described our preadoptive status. It took a lot more courage to walk around our neighborhood and tell people in person that we were now preadoptive and changing Cecilia's name. Some people seemed shocked that we would change a child's name. This is a controversial subject in the adoption world. However, some experts state that until the age of two, children are called by many pet names and haven't internalized their name, so a name change isn't thought of as harmful to the child (Michaels 2002, 48).

One day, I ran into an acquaintance at a coffee shop and as she clutched her own baby in her arms, she said with her eyes wide, "How is she adjusting to the name change?"

I replied, "She is fine—I don't think she has really noticed."

I was surprised by the question, partly because this woman was clearly upset by our changing Cecilia's name—but this seemed like a microdetail of a macrosituation that entailed a child's whole life changing. Considering the enormity of the situation, the woman seemed focused on an insignificant detail. Some day, Cecilia might be angry and change her name back—but this was not going to ruin her life. However, perhaps the name change was a synecdoche for outsiders; it emphasized the awkwardness of the upheaval to them.

One of the reasons it took a lot of courage to change Cecilia's name was because, while it seemed most likely that we would end up adopting, we knew it would be a long haul. It was still a gamble, albeit a pretty safe one. A relative could suddenly appear and say that they were never informed of Cecilia's birth or placement in foster care. The family court judge could counter the agency's recommendation and decide not to terminate the birth mother's rights. Although these things were very unlikely, they could happen.

Another reason it took a lot of courage is because it is pretty unusual for people to change names. The initial use of "Ella" seemed awkward—although not much more so than the initial use of "Peter" and "Martha" when they were just born. It always seems to take a while for a name to seem right for a person. And of course, we spent at least a month correcting people as they continued to call her Cecilia, Cece, and Kiki. During this month, I also went on the Internet to find and order a copy of the baby book I had bought the year before and recopied all that I had written using her new name.

While I told the agency that we had started to call Cecilia Ella, and I explained to the birth family that we had a dog named Cece at home and therefore it caused confusion, everyone continued to call the baby Cecilia. I am sure they disapproved of our changing her name, and I wouldn't be surprised if ACS or the agency had a policy against name changes prior to adoptions. We were the only adoptive parents of Cecilia or her half sisters to do so, although she was also the youngest. I understood why the agency employees and the family members continued to use "Cecilia," although no one ever addressed the subject with me and it made me a little uncomfortable. When I took her to the pediatrician, I would sign her in as "Cecilia ____ (Ella Gerstenzang)." I didn't like this dual identity issue but there was no way around it. I sometimes wondered if Ella ever noticed, and I hoped it didn't affect her in any bad way. (Later, when she had just turned two, I asked, "Who is Cecilia?" She hesitated for just a second and replied, "Ella!" That relieved me of my anxiety because she seemed completely clear that Cecilia and Ella were one and the same.)

At the beginning of January, Martha wanted to bring Ella into her second-grade class on her "share" day. The night before, I was nervous and as Michael and I were going to sleep, I asked what he thought I should do if the kids started asking about Ella's birth family. Michael thought I was worrying too much but we talked about some possible answers—"Sometimes Moms can't take care of kids because they are sick or have problems that are hard to solve"—practicing them to see how they sounded.

The next day on the way to school I asked Martha if she wanted me to introduce Ella and she said, "No, I will." The kids were already sitting on the floor in a circle when we came in, late.

When it was her turn, Martha stood in her spot in the circle, holding Ella's hands. She said: "This is my sister, Ella. She can walk if you hold her hands. She likes music like 'Who Let the Dogs Out.'" Martha sang a verse to demonstrate. "She also likes 'If You're Happy and You Know It,' and she'll clap her hands. She knows some words like 'apple' and 'Mama.'"

At which point, Martha's friend Dominique shouted out, "She's a baby genius!"

The kids all crowded around to get close to Ella and then spontaneously burst into song: "If you're happy and you know it, clap your hands." It was like something from a Disney movie. I was choked with emotion. I was proud of Martha and impressed with her confident presentation and overwhelmed by the unquestioning acceptance of Ella as Martha's sister.

So by the beginning of 2001, as Ella turned one, the agency was clear that the permanency goal had been changed from "reunification" to "adoption." They clarified with ACS that we were the preadoptive parents and addressed with them why Ella would not be placed with one of her half sisters. I asked that the agency file the due diligence on the birth father now. "Due diligence" simply means documenting that they have tried to track down the father to no avail.

I called Ella's law guardian to make sure that she was in agreement with the plan. When the case came before the judge, the agency would be represented by a lawyer, as would ACS and the birth mother. In addition, the legal guardian would also be there as Ella's legal representative. She expressed some hesitation that our preadoptive status might not be in Ella's best interest. I said: "You obviously need to come to your own conclusions. But *I* need to know now what your position is for Cecilia's sake and the sake of my children, my husband, and myself." The guardian said that she thought it might be better for Cecilia to be with one of her half sisters. I said that we planned to keep the relationship open with the birth family. After some discussion, she said that she would support the agency's decision, that is, she said, "There doesn't seem to be any compelling reason to move her." During the conversation, the guardian seemed detached and theoretical and of course, this wasn't surprising, as she had never even met Ella. It was sobering to hear how long the process for adoption would take. It felt like we had done so much work to come up with a permanent plan, but it would be at least a year before the multiple court dates were over.

The agency reduced the frequency of visits to the minimum required—twice a month. When they did this, I requested that they also make some changes to improve the visits for Ella—perhaps working with Zuri to structure the time better. The caseworker suggested that I should sit in on the visits to help Ella feel more relaxed. I started doing this, and while it was awkward at first, over time I enjoyed getting to know the other girls better and developing a better relationship with Zuri. Sometimes, in a pinch, I was left to supervise the visit when the caseworker had to tend to something else. Mostly, I just sat quietly and watched the interaction while Ella sat on my lap.

On February 28, 2001, a milestone passed: Ella had now lived with us for one year. We now had legal protection as the first adoptive resource. On May 29, 2001, exactly fifteen months after Cecilia had come into foster care, the agency lawyers filed a court petition to terminate the birth mother's parental rights. However, it would be another six months, the end of November, before the case would come before a judge.

While it was difficult for us to be stuck in this holding pattern, it could have been much worse. Family court in New York City in the best of times is an overwhelmed institutional system, but in 2001, court-appointed lawyers had gone *fifteen* years without a pay raise and, in protest of this injustice, had stopped accepting new assignments. New York State ranked forty-ninth in the nation in terms of pay for its court-appointed lawyers. The Legal Aid Society provides law guardians for the children in foster care. But their parents, the majority of whom cannot afford a lawyer, have one appointed by the court. If the parents don't have a lawyer, the cases can't proceed. "While family courts everywhere are struggling," Professor Guggenheim, a law professor at New York

University was quoted in the newspaper as saying, New York is "at the extreme end of a dysfunctional system in this country" (Mansnerus, 10 March 2001).

Over the summer, when Ella was one and a half, I saw an article in the *New York Times* entitled, "Man Gets 3-Year Term for Dog's Death." It caught my attention because I remembered the incident in the news the same month that Ella had arrived, February 2000. In a fit of road rage, a man in California had thrown a small dog into traffic and the dog was killed. While I was disturbed by the incident (in fact, the murdered dog even happened to be the same breed as our own family dog), I was stunned that the case had been resolved so quickly compared to our own court case. And in fact, we were lucky, because we were not birth parents checking off the passing months while waiting to be reunified with our child. As foster parents, we had Ella at home with us while we waited.

Sometime between November 2000, when we were identified as preadoptive parents, and November 2001, when we had the first hearing for the termination of parental rights, I stopped referring to us as Ella's "foster parents." Depending on the situation, I would use "preadoptive" (at her new day care, for example) or "adoptive" (with strangers). The simple change in the way we identified ourselves had a dramatic effect on the questions people asked; most stopped asking about where she came from and about her birth family. I don't know whether people are more comfortable with the idea of adoption than with foster care or are less comfortable asking because defining our permanent attachment made it clearer that our family boundary of privacy included Ella as well.

There were exceptions. One day in the summer, my friend Katherine and I planned to meet with our children, who are the same age, in front of the park in her neighborhood. As we stood there saying hello, another friend of Katherine's walked by and stopped to talk. Katherine introduced us: "This is one of Charlie's two unique friends—Ella—and her mother, Sarah. The other has two moms." This statement was followed by stunned silence. I was thinking, Did she really just say that? After the other friend walked away, Katherine said, "Do you think that I shouldn't have said that?" I said I thought she had made us all a bit uncomfortable but it wasn't worth dwelling on.

Katherine often blurted out what I suspect other people only thought about. Her candor could be disconcerting and refreshing. She would ask if I felt overwhelmed by a third child—and just as I would feel defensive, she would say that her very active third child sometimes made her question her decision to have him. I liked how she could say that—it made me feel normal that I sometimes felt overwhelmed, although Ella was a lot easier on me than Charlie was on Katherine. At a year and a half, he was already able to climb out of his bed in the early morning, so Katherine had to put netting over the crib to keep him safe. He was an active, agile little boy who scampered on and out of everything. Ella, on the other hand, loved to sleep in. When she woke up at a very reasonable seven or eight o'clock, she did so slowly. I would peek through the door watching her lie completely relaxed, slowly blinking her eyes and looking around her crib. Eventually, she would reach for a book from the basket I had hung on the side of her crib and begin "reading" to herself.

Later, as we pushed the strollers side by side on the sidewalk, Katherine asked me about what was happening with Ella and then apologized. "I'm sorry, I know you said that it bothers you that people are constantly asking about your feelings." I had a little epiphany at that moment. "You know," I replied, "it doesn't bother me anymore." I realized that it wasn't people's nosiness that had bothered me as much as the excruciating ambivalence of the situation and our uncertain role. It was as if people had been constantly touching a wound and that wound was now healed, so touching it didn't hurt anymore. Now that our role was clear, I could answer questions directly.

Finally on Tuesday, November 27, 2001, I headed off to Manhattan Family Court for the hearing on the termination of parental rights, feeling incredibly nervous. I carried a yellow envelope stuffed with anything that might be remotely useful. The package of paper somehow made me feel more secure, but it was all a bit pointless because I had no legal standing as a foster parent. Although I was allowed to attend, I was told several times that most foster parents don't bother (perhaps because they are discouraged from doing so). Included in the pile was the name and phone number of the law guardian, whom Ella and I had traveled to see the week before for the first time. She was at least the third lawyer assigned to Ella's case and the first to meet Ella or me.

I had taken Ella to downtown Brooklyn to the legal guardian's office for our meeting. I made sure that Ella was dressed up—but not so dressed up that it looked like I was putting on a show. When we were called from the waiting room, the guardian and a social worker brought us to a small office, where Ella sort of slumped on my lap. I talked about how great she was doing— speaking in sentences since she was eighteen months old. They nodded politely and asked if I could leave the room so that they could speak to "Cecilia" in private. I went to the hallway to wait. They came out of the office to get me and when I reentered, I saw Ella sitting on the plastic chair—looking very small and shy by herself. They said that she would not say a word. I realized then that perhaps she wasn't feeling well. And in fact, she wasn't; by the time we got home, she had a slight fever. Although I hadn't known what they wanted from the interview, I felt somehow that we hadn't performed at our best.

❖

Outside the court, there was an enormous line winding around the building due to a security check inside (this was less than three months after 9/11, and the family court building was within walking distance of the World Trade Center site). I ran into Stella, our third social worker, outside the building, and as we waited in line, she told me that she had spent the weekend reviewing the details of the case. She seemed incredibly nervous. This surprised me because I always felt I was the only one who was nervous—as if maybe I was the only one who cared enough to be nervous. I said, "This must be really stressful for you." She said that it was and although she hated to say it, sometimes it was easier if the birth parents didn't show up because testifying about their non-compliant behavior in front of them is difficult. Stella said with feeling, "You know, I have to *work* with these parents." It dawned on me how difficult it must be to work with the foster parents and birth parents simultaneously.

Stella also explained to me that the termination of parental rights has two parts. The first part is the fact finding, where the agency (through testimony by the social worker) presents the facts of the case. The second part is the decision-making, or dispositional, stage. Stella said that it was very unlikely from her experience that the hearing would move beyond the fact-finding stage that day.

Once inside the building, after winding through another line, we had to empty our pockets and go through a metal detector. I must have looked as anxious as I felt because as the cop gave me back my things after I cleared the metal detector, he gave me a nice smile and said, "You did a good job." To get up to the ninth floor, we had to take an elevator. The elevators were so crowded that it took at least ten minutes before I even attempted to get on one. On the ninth floor, the building was a lot more pleasant with plenty of wooden benches to sit on and large windows that let in lots of light.

I saw Zuri and her boyfriend and gave them some pictures I had taken on a recent visit. They had come out particularly well—most of the pictures were of the new baby Cecilia's/Ella's mother had given birth to a few months earlier. The two of them spent the next half-hour looking at the same eight pictures. I wondered if they had any other pictures of their new baby boy, who had also been placed in foster care. I couldn't help watching them out of the corner of my eye. They were smiling, laughing at some pictures and talking about the kids. And as much as I wanted to move on with my own life, I couldn't quite believe that we were all assembled to terminate forever this woman's rights as a parent to Ella.

While waiting for the case to begin, I met the lawyer for the agency, Arthur. He was pleasant and seemed knowledgeable. He said he was going to see if the birth mother would consider surrendering her rights. Stella murmured that this was "unlikely." Arthur wanted to know if I would commit to set visits with the birth mother, and I said we always intended to keep an open relationship with the birth family. However, I also knew that whatever I agreed to and whatever my good intentions were, once the adoption was finalized, the visits were not enforceable by law. Arthur approached the birth mother's lawyer, Kathy (who had just met the birth mother for the first time), and made his pitch. Kathy then spoke to Zuri. During this conversation, I was a nervous wreck, crossing my fingers in a superstitious attempt to influence the conversation. When the birth mother and her lawyer finished speaking, Zuri looked angry. She then related the conversation to her boyfriend. They spoke intensely—huddled together in a bit of private space over by a window. I overheard her say in an impatient tone, "I am not a robot!"

At 11:00 A.M. (our appointment was for 9:30), we were called into the courtroom. On the way in, Arthur whispered to me that Zuri had declined to surrender her rights. The judge sat up high at her desk in the front center of the room. Next to her were the stenographer and the witness chair. Facing the judge were two long tables in a semi-circle, each with at least six chairs. Behind these chairs were more chairs along the back wall. It was my first time in a courtroom, and it looked more or less like one on television. I sat in a chair along the wall, behind the agency lawyer, social worker, and law guardian. Zuri and her lawyer sat at the other table. The proceedings began with the agency lawyer questioning the social worker in depth about every attempt made to help the birth mother. The lawyer asked if the agency had provided referrals to the parenting and drug rehabilitation classes that the judge ordered the birth mother to attend.

"Where was the referral made?" the lawyer wanted to know. "On what date? And what happened? Did the agency ask the birth mother why she was not attending the required services? Did the agency make another attempt to refer the birth mother to services?" And so on.

I wanted to ask, "If the birth mother did go to all the required classes, would she be able to parent appropriately?"

While this courtroom looked somewhat like one on television, the tenor of the proceedings was different from a TV drama, where there is an intellectual intensity to the witness questions and cross-examinations. This seemed more pro forma—going through the motions to establish that the birth mother had not met any of the requirements. Stella seemed nervous but organized. I was impressed by how the agency seemed to meet every requirement to help the birth parent and with the thoroughness of the documentation. It dawned on me how important this was—if there were no documentation, there would be no case. I decided it had been worth the trips from Brooklyn to Manhattan and back to work with this agency for what now seemed like a very important aspect of quality social work. In *Child Welfare and the Law*, Theodore Stein refers to the case records kept by the social workers as the "core of the information network." He notes that these records are often the only constant as a client moves through the child-welfare system with ever-changing caseworkers (Stein 1998, 273).

During the testimony, the judge appeared to be skimming a newspaper. I couldn't believe it and neither could Arthur, who leaned back in his chair during one of Stella's lengthy responses to his questions and whispered to me, "Do you see what she is reading?" On the one hand, I could sympathize, as I often feel like knitting during long meetings, and I could tell by the judge's questions that she was paying close attention. But on the other hand—how disrespectful to all of us!

After about an hour of testimony, the judge said that she had a twelve o'clock appointment and therefore the case must be adjourned. I was really dismayed. After all these months, finally everyone was in the same place, the case was proceeding, and it was all being wrapped up after only one hour! I had to resist the impulse to stand up and protest. The lawyers and the judge took out their calendars and, after some discussion, settled on another date to continue, at the end of February, three months away.

At the very end, Zuri's lawyer asked the judge to order the visits between her client and her child to be weekly. While for the first year visits between Ella and her mother had been every week, once the permanency goal changed from return to mother to adoption, the agency reduced the visits to once every two weeks, the minimum required by New York State law. The judge basically said, "Why not?" and looked to Stella to respond. This was a low moment for me; I was already reeling from the news that we would live in limbo for another three months, and now it seemed that I would have to start taking Ella in for weekly visits again. Stella seemed caught off-guard but responded that in this case, it seemed in the child's best interest to have bimonthly visits. The judge just left it at that.

I left the courtroom furious with the birth mother for not surrendering her rights. I was so upset and disappointed that the hearing was not completed. We could not move on to adoption until the birth mother's rights were terminated. I felt caught in a trap—early in the day, I thought I could see the exit, but when I got closer, it was just another corner to turn. However, by later that day, while I remained discouraged that the situation was not resolved, my anger melted and I actually felt respect for Zuri, sticking up for what she believed was right and for not being intimidated.

At the beginning of December, I had a telephone conversation with Stella, who told me that the social work teams had to be switched around and we were going to have yet another new social worker. She was apologetic and said that she would continue on the court case until it was finished, for which I was grateful. Stella also clarified with me how long Ella had lived with us. Stella said that if a child had been in care for more than eighteen months, the child was considered "hard to place" and when the child was adopted, the family would receive a stipend. In this case, it would be about the same as the foster care stipend, approximately five hundred dollars a month. Ironically, we were going to receive this stipend because the court system was so slow. I felt awkward about accepting this money and I told Stella that while I understood we were entitled to it, if it fell through for some reason, it wasn't important to us.

While I think it is important to continue stipends for children—for many families it might make the difference in their ability to adopt or not—I had often wondered whether the labels made the children less attractive to potential adoptive families. "Hard-to-place" and "special needs" can mean that the child is part of a sibling group (two or more siblings in New York State), is over a certain age (defined in New York State as ten years and older if the child is white and eight years and older if the child is a member of a minority group), is a member of a minority group, or has a heath issue. The labels sound intimidating. Of course, there are a certain percentage of children in foster care who would be very challenging to parent, but that doesn't mean they and countless others aren't lovable or able to love an adoptive family.

I mentioned to Stella that someday I would like to look at the full case record. I said that as Ella's parent, I felt that it was my responsibility to learn as much as I could about her birth family. Stella said she understood, but all records are confidential, kept even from the children themselves. I believe she said that it was a liability issue for the agency. I was dismayed to hear that children in foster care and their parents are not entitled to records about their own lives. Again we were lucky, because we at least had been with Ella for most of her life; for children who have been in multiple placements, it seemed very unfair.

In December 2001 and January 2002, the two months following our hour in court (for which we had waited six months), the media paid some attention to the plight of U.S. families attempting to adopt children from Vietnam and Cambodia. When asked to issue visas so that the children could be brought to the United States, the INS found improprieties that they felt they needed to investigate, such as concerns that birth parents hadn't properly or willingly relinquished their rights. The news program *20/20* did a story on the issue and several prominent politicians spoke up on the families' behalf: "They say this agency isn't doing things correctly. I say, 'Fine, investigate,'" said Chuck Schumer, the senator from New York State. "But don't hold these families in limbo." When I called Senator Schumer's office to ask if he wouldn't mind giving the same attention to children "in limbo" in his own state, I was told that "he would get my message."

On Thursday, February 21, 2002, Peter, Martha, Ella, and I went for dinner at Inaka. It was almost two years to the day that we went to Inaka while waiting for Ella (who was then Cecilia) to arrive. Ella was now two years old and no longer a baby. She had just been potty trained and went to the restaurant happily wearing her new Valentine underpants. She was also now quite verbal and as we prepared to leave the house, she said, "I don't want my stroller. I want to walk." Which she did, there and back.

While Ella was busy growing and thriving, our court proceedings dragged on. The previous week, our neighbor died, a youthful eighty-five-year-old woman of whom I was very fond. Not only would I miss her but also I felt sad that she died without knowing that Ella was adopted. She often asked me over our garden fences about the proceedings, and once she expressed her concern that we were so attached to Ella when something could still go wrong. I had tried to confidently reassure her that it would all come to pass.

The following week was the second hearing on termination of parental rights (TPR), and I once again felt myself getting excited and anxious. I tried to steel myself against the crushing disappointment that nothing would happen. By this time, at the agency's suggestion we had hired a lawyer to represent us in the eventual adoption. Coincidentally, we hired the husband of the teaching assistant from my research class at Columbia University, who had met Ella the day after she arrived at our house. It was a relief to hire a lawyer because even though nothing had changed, it felt as if we were making progress. It was also great to have someone who seemed to know the system as *our* advocate. Although the termination of parental rights hadn't happened yet, we began to collect the paperwork for the adoption. After all we had been required to do for the foster care system, this seemed like a breeze.

As the date neared for the second TPR hearing, I became increasingly worried that one of the parties to the case wouldn't show up and that the case would have to be postponed. I had heard about this happening on numerous occasions from other foster parents and social workers. We had waited three months for this date and I didn't want to wait another three months or more. I called the agency social worker to confirm the time and the date. I also called our attorney. He said that it wasn't necessary for him to attend but if asked I should say that we had retained counsel and that we were ready to file the petition for adoption. I called the law guardian and she said she was all set. She said that she just hoped that the birth mother's attorney showed up.

At 9:00 AM, on Tuesday, February 26, 2002, I took the subway to lower Manhattan to the Manhattan Family Court building. This time as I exited the subway, I knew in which direction to walk and in fact I could see the building from several blocks away. From my previous experience, I knew that I might be a while so I stopped at a stand to buy a cinnamon raisin bagel with butter and a decaf coffee. I would have liked a regular coffee but decided that I was anxious enough already.

When I got up to the ninth floor, the first person I saw was the birth mother's attorney. That was a real relief. I could see the two social workers from the agency sitting together on a waiting-room bench. One of the social workers, Linda, was newer and the other, Stella, was the one who had testified at the previous hearing in November. They waved to me and I went over and sat with them. Stella again was clearly nervous. I told her that I was nervous as well, although I had very little part to play. About twenty minutes later, Zuri and her boyfriend came in. They came over and we said hello and made some small talk about some other members of the birth mother's family.

That is the funny thing about foster care. By the time we got to this point, almost two years and approximately fifty meetings later, Zuri and I were cordially acquainted. We had met each other's mothers and sisters. While there was little depth to our relationship and I am sure an underlying distrust on the birth mother's part, we had a comfortable way of communicating. While I would have never been able to see this from the start, I now felt that it was an enormous benefit for everyone. I hoped it provided Zuri with some comfort to know that Ella lived with a family who loved her. Initially the thought of having this relationship would have been so intimidating, I would have never considered it unless forced to do so. And although Michael and I planned to stay in contact with the birth family, if we should lose touch over the years, I would hold information for Ella about her birth family in my memory for when she wanted to access it. I came to see the development of this relationship as a healthy and unwitting benefit of the foster care system.

However, I was now more than ready to move on. As our eleven o'clock court time neared, I became more anxious and stopped reading the newspaper because I was rereading the same sentences without grasping their meaning. The agency lawyer, Anne, came over to speak with the social workers and make sure they were prepared. She was a colleague of Arthur's, the attorney who had come to the last hearing. Arthur had asked her the previous afternoon if she would take over the case. I was introduced to Anne, who asked me if I would like to testify during the dispositional phase. I said, "Sure, if it helps." Anne said that making the decision that termination of parental rights is in the child's best interest is stressful for judges, and it is her opinion that knowing the child will be adopted into a loving home can make the decision easier for a judge. After she walked away, I said to Stella that the last-minute switch in attorneys wasn't very confidence inspiring. Stella assured me that Anne was an excellent attorney and that we were in great hands.

Shortly after eleven, we were called into the courtroom. This time I sat up at the table, facing slightly to the left of the judge with the social workers and the lawyer from the agency on my left. Sitting to my right were the law guardian and her supervisor. Zuri sat at the table facing slightly to the right of the judge, all by herself. Her lawyer was nowhere to be seen. We all stood when asked and stated our name and relationship to the case ("Sarah Gerstenzang, foster mother"), raised our right hands, and swore to tell the truth. The court officer was sent to find the birth mother's attorney and came back to say that she was presenting another case. The lawyer from the agency, Anne, then suggested to the judge that we postpone until 2:30 that afternoon when Anne was supposed to have another case go before this judge that she knew was not going to take place. We were all asked if we could stay until the afternoon and it was confirmed that the birth mother's attorney would be available then. I felt so grateful that this lawyer had thought of this solution and would have cleared the rest of the week, if necessary, to finish this task.

As we left the courtroom, Anne offered to take the social workers and me to lunch after she took care of another case. Linda had to go back to the agency office but Anne, Stella, and I agreed to meet in front of the court building at one o'clock. Stella spent the next hour reviewing her notes. I spent my time calling Michael to give him a minute-by-minute account. As I walked through the waiting area, I saw Zuri and her boyfriend. I wondered if they had money for lunch and considered offering them some but felt awkward and unsure so I didn't. When I met Stella, at one o'clock, she mentioned that she had had the same thought and did give them money for lunch.

At 2:30, we were assembled in the waiting room. Anne reported to us that an adoption was taking place but that we would be next. She said to me: "Adoptions always take precedence. Some day you will appreciate that." Sure enough, about fifteen minutes later, a sweet little brown boy about four years old and dressed in a tie and jacket walked out of the courtroom with his Hispanic adoptive mother, who was beaming and weeping. The mother had her camera and several shots were taken of the mother and son, lawyer and social worker. It was a moving scene.

In the meantime, in another part of the waiting room, the birth mother's lawyer, Kathy, told the agency lawyer that she would have to postpone again because she was now on another matter, before a referee (an attorney who acts as a mediator). As Anne reported to us afterward, she told Kathy that she was sure Kathy was aware that judges take precedence over referees and that she was prepared to report this to the judge. Kathy acquiesced. She would be available.

So shortly after three o'clock, we reassembled in the court-room before the judge. My heart thumping, I tried to sit still because my chair squeaked if I moved. Kathy cross-examined Stella. Kathy's main defense strategy focused on how I had interfered with Cecilia's ability to bond with her mother by being present in the family visits during the second year Cecilia lived with us. It wasn't a very effective defense but it certainly took me off-guard. I thought: Is this all my fault? Am I the reason this baby is living with us and not her birth mother? I felt very defensive. I recalled hearing social workers talk about foster parents "sabotaging" the relationship between birth parents and their children, as if the foster parents are to blame. Then I thought about how I had sat in on the visits because Ella needed me there, how I had tried to be as inconspicuous as possible, and how, if Ella hadn't been distressed, I would have much preferred to be reading my book in the waiting room.

As before, Stella was careful to check her records, which filled binders in two large canvas bags, if she was unsure of an exact date or referral that had been made. Anne then got up and redirected, to clarify any details that seemed to get muddled in the numerous questions. I was riveted by the exchanges but also kept covertly checking my watch and the clock on the wall because I was afraid time would run out again. A few times I looked over at the birth mother and as I stared at her profile, I was struck by how her head shape was so similar to Ella's.

After the fact-finding was finished, the dispositional phase began. After Stella testified, I was called to the stand.

"Could you please state for the record who lives in your household and your ages?" Anne said.

"Myself, my husband, Michael, we are both thirty-seven. Our son, Peter, who is eleven and our daughter, Martha, who is eight. And Cecilia, who is two."

"And what do you and your husband do for a living?"

"Michael is a lawyer and I am a social worker."

She asked how many bedrooms we had and if Cecilia had her own bedroom. This really made me squirm because I felt that she was implying that our financial situation would make us better parents. I thought of the tiny apartment we moved to when my mother left my father, where my three sisters and I shared two bedrooms and my mother slept on a small back porch. Anne asked how long we had had Cecilia and if we intended to adopt her. She asked the nature of the relationship between Cecilia and my birth children. I said, "siblinglike."

The legal guardian then got up and said, "Mrs. Gerstenzang, you have described your relationship with the child to me. Could you please do so for the court?"

I paused to search for the words. "I love her. I have cared for her from the age of five weeks." I did not look at the birth mother; I focused on the lawyer. "We have raised her just like our two older children."

"And your husband?" she asked.

"He feels the same."

No one had further questions or testimony, so the judge made her determination. "There is clear and convincing evidence that this mother has permanently neglected this child by failing to plan for her future. I hearby remand custody of this child to the _____ Agency and the Commissioner of Social Services of the City of New York."

I sat in my chair, stunned and oblivious to everything around me. After several minutes, the court officer announced, "You may clear the courtroom."

I went to the waiting room, where the agency lawyer informed me that the TPR paperwork had to be filed with the court, which would take six to eight weeks. She also told me we could file our adoption papers simultaneously. After she left, I spoke briefly with the social worker. We agreed that although it was difficult to hear all the evidence in support of the determination of permanent neglect, in another way it was cathartic to feel certain that the right decision was made. I said, "I thought that this moment was going to be bittersweet, but you know, it feels just pretty sweet." I was surprised by my lack of empathy for the horribleness of the moment for the birth mother. My being used as the reason for the birth mother's inadequate parenting probably didn't help my sense of empathy. I know that I will always carry a feeling of sadness and even guilt for her, but this moment was the beginning of us *really* being Ella's parents, and that felt joyful. I was euphoric on the way home, ready to move on with my life with my family.

The End of the Beginning

THE COURT had terminated the rights of Ella's birth parents. She was now a "legal orphan." However, we couldn't move on just yet. The final step would be adoption. Over the next months, I was still obligated to bring Ella to the agency for visits as I had been doing for the past two years. Ella was quiet during the visits and stuck to me like glue, spending most of the visits on my lap, which was unusual for her, since she was normally very active. She didn't pay too much attention to Zuri—Zuri herself was more focused on her youngest child—but closely watched the other kids. Once when I was packing up a bag on a Wednesday afternoon, Ella said she didn't want to go to "Dawn's house," meaning the agency. Dawn was sometimes aggressive toward Ella, I think because she was jealous of the attention I gave Ella. I reassured Ella that Dawn would not hurt her, and she went to the visit happily.

While there was no requirement that Ella meet with Zuri, as her rights had been terminated, Ella had to have visits with the older half sisters who were not yet adopted and the younger half brother who was in foster care. However, since no one had any objection to Zuri's attending the visits and because she was entitled to visits with her son, the visits were kept open to everyone. I resented that the visits were not scheduled at times convenient for me or Ella. I would think about how much more I (and, I think, Ella) would enjoy the experience if we could have met everyone in the park on a weekday morning. This was not practical though because of the older girls' school schedules. I was now working part-time and I had to hire a babysitter to pick up Ella at day care, bring her to Manhattan, and meet me at the agency every other Wednesday. Then the babysitter had to head back to Brooklyn in time to pick up Peter and Martha from afterschool by 6:00 PM.

As the weeks passed that spring, my reluctance must have become more obvious. One day in the middle of May, I got a call at work from Ella's day care saying that she was ill. The teacher asked me to leave work to come and pick her up. After picking her up that afternoon, I called the agency and let them know that we wouldn't be able to come to that evening's visit. The next day at work, I received an e-mail from the social worker stating that she wanted me to fax her a copy of the doctor's diagnosis confirming Cecilia's illness, so that she could show it to ACS. I was furious, because I felt she was implying that I was lying—and this after I had to leave work early the day before. E-mailing with the social workers was a new thing for me. Either it had just become apparent to me that this was a possibility or it was only recently that they had this capability in their office. Anyway, it suited me to communicate in this fashion with this new and fourth social worker. I was tired of building personal relationships, and I was counting the days until the adoption.

I e-mailed back without my usual first-name salutation:

Ms. Hernandez,
The message that I left was that Ella's school called me to pick her up early on Wednesday because the teachers felt that she wasn't well. They suspected that she had an ear infection because she said that her ear was hurting. I did not take her to the doctor because although she was very crabby on Wednesday afternoon, when she woke up on Thursday, she seemed much better. If you or ACS would like to call her day care to confirm this, feel free to do so.
Sarah Gerstenzang

In June our agency moved to the Bronx; New York City was shifting to a new system in which foster care services would be neighborhood based. Agencies had to be located in their allocated districts and provide foster homes to children in the neighborhoods that they came from. This made the idea of attending visits more overwhelming, because the Bronx is much farther away, and my interactions with the social worker became tense once again. At the same time, we were told that the date for Ella's adoption was set for the beginning of September. We had only two months to go, and Michael pleaded with me to do whatever the agency asked. He took Ella to one visit that we arranged ourselves at a park in northern Manhattan. I took Ella and Martha to the next one up in the Bronx. It was over ninety degrees that day and it took us almost two hours by subway. When we arrived, no one else had showed up. The social worker and I waited awkwardly together as the minutes passed. Finally, she said that we might as well go, as it seemed that no one else was coming. She was apologetic and she looked nervous that I might be upset. I said: "Look, these things happen and I know it isn't your fault. But we aren't coming again." On the way home, Martha held Ella's hand to get on the train, as I had the stroller that I had just carried down the steps. As Ella was stepping on the train, one of her legs fell in the gap between the train and the platform—she went straight down, pulling Martha to the floor at the doorway to the train. Immediately, other passengers picked them up and brought them safely on to the train as the doors closed. It was very frightening, and Martha and Ella both burst into tears while I fought mine back.

We looked forward with excitement and nervousness to the adoption, which was now set for September 10, 2002. This date was almost a year to the day after 9/11, and our anxiety about that first anniversary of the most traumatic day of our lives was omnipresent. Michael and I did not want to be sucked into the fear we had felt the year before. However as the weather began to change at the beginning of September, our minds were unwillingly brought back to that month the year before. We didn't need to look at a calendar, we could just glance at our garden and see the slightly spent growth, the brown tinges on the edges of some leaves, and we knew what time of year it was.

We focused on our excitement, although at times—because of all we had been through and because we were repeatedly warned that last-minute delays happen frequently and can hold up adoptions for months—we tried to keep it in check. We went with relish to the invitation store to pick out announcements, but we asked that the announcements not be printed until we called to say that the adoption had actually been completed. As we sorted through the books of cards that we could choose from, the clerk asked what country our adopted daughter was from. I replied, "Brooklyn!" We planned a party for mid-October and decided that we would hold it regardless of whether the adoption happened. We bought gifts for the kids to celebrate—gold charm bracelets for Martha and Ella and for Peter a piece of jade on a red thread that could be worn as a necklace. The woman at the shop in Chinatown where we purchased the gifts said that jade was prized for its "human" element, as it takes on the warmth of the person wearing it. I hid the gifts away in my dresser drawer.

At last, the day of Ella's adoption arrived. Peter and Martha left for school, gleeful that the date had fallen on a school day because they would leave school at noon and be able to share the excitement with their friends. Michael seemed to feel the same way about going to work—just the day before he had come home with two little t-shirts for Ella that one of his clients, who also had an adopted child, had sent from Switzerland.

The adoption was scheduled for 2:00 PM. At about 11:00 AM, I started to get dressed. Ella was already wearing her best dress. She followed me everywhere, first to the sink so I could shave my underarms—she ran to get her plastic razor so she could pretend to do the same. Then to my bedroom as I put on my black-and-white-checked dress. It amused me to think about how one gets dressed up for an adoption and how one sheds clothes for a birth. I got goose bumps for just a moment as I was changing, thinking, *Today* is September 10 and tomorrow is September 11—the amazingly good and the amazingly bad back-to-back like that. I wondered if Ella, at two years and nine months, had any idea about the significance of the day. (A few weeks later, it was confirmed for me that she did not when she asked me: "Why am I getting these presents? Is it my birthday?")

Ella entertained herself in my room, petting the cat's fur in the wrong direction, "She's not going to scratch me though?" She ran her hands through Michael's ties and knocked half of them to the ground. She spotted something under the bed—"Look Mommy! I found some lip scotch!" that is, lip gloss. As my excitement mounted, I put on my necklace with shaking hands. Ella stood by my side, smashing two of my glass paperweights together in a clapping motion. "If you're happy and you know it, clap your hands . . ."

We picked up Peter and Martha at school and took a car service to the family court building in Manhattan. I could see Michael waiting on the corner as we approached. He gave us a big smile when the car pulled up. As we went into the building together, all dressed up, we were as cheerful and excited as if we were leaving on a family vacation. I was the guide showing them all where to go—through the security and up in the elevator to the waiting room. It surprised me to realize I was the only one of us who had been to that building before. It had felt as if we had all gone through the process together. I was somewhat oblivious to the surroundings and the throngs of people—the building felt like my old worn couch to me now. But to Michael and Peter, it was different. Michael thought the surroundings and the people were all a bit worn down. He said it felt like one more visit at the agency. He had wanted the experience to be more personal—the way labor and delivery were separated from the rest of the hospital so all you felt around you was excitement. Peter said the security checks and the seats reminded him of an airport. He had thought it would be more like a courthouse in the movies.

We met our lawyer for the first time in the waiting room shortly before we were called into the courtroom. The actual proceeding took only a few minutes. I had imagined that we would sign our documents with a flourish—I had forgotten that they had been sent to us in the mail and that we had already signed them. After the adoption was declared final, we took some pictures with the judge and left the courtroom as a family.

Afterward, Martha said that she had been both nervous and excited, the way she feels on the first day of school when she doesn't know what to expect. She said that our family didn't feel any different physically but she felt more secure emotionally. "Before, I knew that I could wake up one morning and Ella wouldn't be here."

Epilogue

We adopted Cecilia on September 10, 2002. Her name was officially changed to Ella Lynn Cecilia Gerstenzang. Although the process had seemed to take an eternity to us, the average length of stay for children who are adopted from foster care in New York City is 4.3 years—Ella beat the odds by remaining in foster care for 2.6 years. The agency sent us flowers and a terrific book on adoptive parenting. We were really touched by the thoughtfulness of these two acts. All tensions between us were moot; we sent the social workers a thank-you note telling them how much we appreciated their hard work.

The adoption itself and the sense of security it gave us seemed to deepen our relationship with Ella even further. It felt as if we were finally able to transplant to our garden a beautiful potted plant we had been nurturing, where the roots could spread out and go deep so that there was no limit to how healthy and full that plant could grow.

We have a friend, Bill, who adopted a son from the same agency. After our adoptions were finalized, and he was considering adopting again, we talked about how, as miserable as the process was at times, it had some bizarre appeal. Bill said: "You know, I hate scary extreme sports—I would never skydive or bungee jump, but once you are finished with the foster/adoption process, it gives you what I would imagine to be a similar thrill. Perhaps it is like a marathon, which takes strength and endurance and courage to even attempt it. And for those few who can finish, a tremendous sense of accomplishment." I had to agree. Michael and I had already talked about *if* we had been interested in having a fourth child (which we are not!), we would go through the same process—again not looking to adopt but being open to that option. While we had agonized over the role of race in our adoption, we were now completely comfortable that we had done the right thing.

There is an expression in Yiddish, *bshert*, which means something was meant to be. My father-in-law once referred to our adoption as *bshert*. I feel that there is an incredible "fit" for Ella in our family. She seems to belong with us, and I often wonder what part of her is a result of what she was born with and what part has been influenced by her environment (us). I would like to take a lot of the credit but I believe that she was born with so much; in her I see the strengths of her birth family—her sweet disposition, her empathy for others, and her determination.

It is hard to think of a way to replace the whole foster care system. Sometimes it is necessary to remove children from their birth families, and we need to have a system in place to do so. However, the United States, the wealthiest country in the world, could treat these families so much more respectfully and responsibly. While the government officials entrusted with children in foster care are most often caring, hard-working people, having children "parented" by a government agency, except for a very short length of time, is a completely inadequate idea. Every child needs a parent who is capable and committed to caring for them.

Maybe we weren't the ideal foster parents, in the sense that we were unrealistic about how attached we would become to the child placed in our care. But it was also that personal attachment that drove us to intensely monitor the options for Ella. Sometimes, I think about what might have happened if Ella had left our home to live with Lorraine and then had to move again when Lorraine was decertified as a foster parent. I think how any normal child would have gone berserk with emotional distress and how that, in turn, could have caused Ella to be moved again. This is a path that thousands of children in foster care in the United States have taken. If one thinks of each of those children as an individual, the thought can break your heart.

References

Altstein, H., and McRoy, R. (2000). *Does Family Preservation Serve a Child's Best Interests?* Washington, D.C.: Georgetown University Press.

American Psychiatric Association (1994). *Diagnostic and Statistical Manual of Mental Disorders,* 4th edition. Washington, D.C.: American Psychiatric Association

Banks, I. (2000). *Hair Matters: Beauty, Power, and Black Women's Consciousness.* New York: New York University Press.

Barbell, K., and Freundlich, M. (2001). *Foster Care Today.* Washington, D.C.: Casey Family Programs.

Becker-Weidman, A. (2001, April). "Notes on Attachment." *Fostering Families Today,* 34–35.

Belsky, J. (1993). "Etiology of Child Maltreatment: A Developmental-Ecological Analysis." *Psychological Bulletin* 114, 3:413–34.

Bernstein, N. (2001a). *The Lost Children of Wilder: The Epic Struggle to Change Foster Care.* New York: Pantheon Books.

———. (2001b, July 7). "New York Ranks City's Private Foster Home Programs." *New York Times.*

Borshay Liem, D. (2000). www.pbs.org/pov/firstpersonplural/historical/transracial.html.

Bowlby, J. (1988). *A Secure Base: Parent-Child Attachment and Healthy Human Development.* New York: Basic Books.

Brodzinsky, D. M., Schechter, M. D., and Marantz Henig, R. (1992). *Being Adopted: The Lifelong Search for Self.* New York: Doubleday.

Cahn, K., and Johnson, P. (1993). *Children Can't Wait: Reducing Delays in Out-of-Home Care.* Washington, D.C.: Child Welfare League of America.

Center for Nutrition Policy and Promotion, U.S. Department of Agriculture. *Expenditures on Children by Families 2005 Annual Report.* Miscellaneous publication no. 1528-2005. www.usda.gov/cnpp/using2.html.

Collison, M. N-K. (2002). *It's All Good Hair: The Guide to Styling and Grooming Black Children's Hair.* New York: Harper Collins.

Community Data Profiles. (1998, March). New York City Administration for Children's Services.

Correspondents of the *New York Times* (2001). *How Race Is Lived in America: Pulling Together, Pulling Apart*. New York: Times Books/ Henry Holt.

Cournos, F. (1999). *City of One: a memoir*. New York: Plume.

Crumbley, J. (1999). *Transracial Adoption and Foster Care*. Washington, D.C.: Child Welfare League of America.

Curtis, P. A.; Dale, G., Jr.; and Kendall, J. C. (1999). *The Foster Care Crisis: Translating Research into Policy and Practice*. Lincoln: University of Nebraska Press / Child Welfare League of America.

DiNitto, D. M. (1995). *Social Welfare: Politics and Public Policy*. Boston: Allyn and Bacon.

Dore, M. M. (1993, November). "Family Preservation and Poor Families: When 'Homebuilding' Is Not Enough." *Families in Society*, 545–56.

Fenton, R. (2001). *Adopting a Child in Britain: Advice for Prospective Adopters*. rridley@fenton60.freeserve.co.uk.

Fisher, A. Q. (2001). *Finding Fish: A memoir*. New York: Morrow.

Forman, C. (2002, January/February). "On Becoming African American." *Adoptive Families* 35, 1.

Freundlich, M. (2000a). *Adoption and Ethics: The Market Forces in Adoption*. Washington, D.C.: Child Welfare League of America.

Freundlich, M. (2000b). *Adoption and Ethics: The Role of Race, Culture, and National Origin in Adoption*. Washington, D.C.: Child Welfare League of America.

Gittrich, G. (2000, December 3). "Cure for Empty Nesters: Foster Care Agency Helps to Fill a Growing Need." *New York Daily News*.

Gootman, E. (2002, January 28). "Investigation by I.N.S. Delays Obtaining Visas and Snarls Adoptions in Vietnam." *New York Times*.

Hicks, R. B. (1999). *Adopting in America: How to Adopt within One Year*. Sun City, Calif.: Wordslinger Press.

Holt International (2002, January 22). www.holtinternational.com.

Hopson, D. P., and Hopson, D. S. (1990). *Different and Wonderful: Raising Black Children in a Race-Conscious Society*. New York: Simon and Schuster.

Hrdy, S. B. (1999). *Mother Nature: A History of Mothers, Infants, and Natural Selection*. New York: Pantheon.

Interracial Families (2000, September 11). www.adopting.org/inter.html.

Kinard, T. (1997). *No Lye! The African American Woman's Guide to Natural Hair Care*. New York: St. Martin's Griffin.

Levinson, L. (2000, June 20). "Inside New York's Foster Care System: 34,000 Kids Trying to Catch a Break." *Village Voice*, 41–49.

Lindsay, C. H. (1996). *Nothing Good Ever Happens to Me: An Adoption Love Story*. Washington, D.C.: Child and Family Press.

"Man Gets 3-Year Term for Dog's Death." (2002, July 17). *New York Times*.

Mansnerus, L. (2001, January 17). "A Brake on the Wheels of Justice: Shortage of Lawyers for the Poor Plagues the Courts." *New York Times*.

———. (2001, March 10). "For Lawyers in Family Court, Preparing for Cases Is a Luxury." *New York Times*.

Mansfield, D.F.W. (1993). *Goodbye, Baby Venus*. New York: University Press of America.

McRoy, R. G., and Grape, H. "Skin Color in Transracial and Inracial Adoptive Placements: Implications for Special Needs Adoptions." *Child Welfare* 78, 5:673–92.

McRoy, R. G.; Oglesby, Z.; and Grape, H. (1997). "Achieving Same-Race Adoptive Placements for African American Children: Culturally Sensitive Practice Approaches." *Child Welfare* 76, 1:85–104.

Michaels, J. (2002, January/February). "The Name Game: Adoptive Families," 35, 1:48.

Miniter, R. F. (1998). *The Things I Want Most: The Extraordinary Story of a Boy's Journey to a Family of His Own*. New York: Bantam.

Nash, J. M. (1997, February 3). Fertile Minds. *Time*, 53.

National Association of Black Social Workers (1994). *Preserving African American Families*. Position statement. Detroit: NABSW.

Neff, M. A. (1999). *Adopting Foster Children: A Handbook for Foster Parents*. St. Albans: New York State Foster and Adoptive Parent Association.

O'Brien, P.; Massat, C. R.; and Gleeson, J. P. (2001, November–December). "Upping the Ante: Relative Caregivers' Perceptions of Changes in Child Welfare Policies." *Child Welfare* 80, 6:719–48.

O'Connor, S. (2001). *Orphan Trains: The Story of Charles Loring Brace and the Children He Saved and Failed*. New York: Houghton Mifflin.

Pasztor, E. M., and Wynne, S. F. (1995). *Foster Parent Retention and Recruitment: The State of the Art in Practice and Policy*. Washington, D.C.: Child Welfare League of America.

Patton, S. (2000). *Birthmarks: Transracial Adoption in Contemporary America*. New York: New York University Press.

Raible, J. (1990). "The Significance of Racial Identity in Transracially Adopted Young Adults." www.nysccc.org/T-Rarts/raible.html (accessed 2002, April 2).

Richards, K. N. (1998). *Tender Mercies: Inside the World of a Child Abuse Investigator*. Washington, D.C.: Child Welfare League of America.

Roberts, D. (2002). *Shattered Bonds: The Color of Child Welfare*. New York: Basic Civitas.

Roche, T. (2000, November 13). "The Shame of Foster Care: The Crisis of Foster Care." *Time*, 74–82.

Saint Louis, C. (2001, April 15). "What They Were Thinking." *New York Times Magazine*, 24.

Sameroff, A. J. (1986). "Environmental Context of Child Development." *Annual Progress in Child Psychiatry and Development* 109, 1:192–200.

Sengupta, S. (2000, September 22). "Drawn to the Faces Others Avoid: For Some, Foster Care System Fulfills a Longing to Adopt." *New York Times*.

Sheehan, S. (1993). *Life for Me Ain't Been No Crystal Stair: One Family's Passage through the Child Welfare System*. New York: Vintage.

Solinger, R. (2001). *Beggars and Choosers: How the Politics of Choice Shapes Adoption, Abortion, and Welfare in the United States*. New York: Hill and Wang.

Stein, T. J. (1998). *Child Welfare and the Law*. Revised ed. Washington, D.C.: CWLA Press.

Suleiman, L. (2002, March). "Racial Representation in Child Victim and Foster Care Populations, State Summary Data by Race." Data collected from Child Welfare Outcomes 1999: Annual Report, USDHHS, ACF/ACYF, Children's Bureau; U.S. Department of Commerce, Bureau of the Census; U. S. Department of Health and Human Services, ACF/ACYF, Children's Bureau, NCANDS Summary Data and; U. S. Department of Health and Human Services, ACF/ACYF, Children's Bureau AFCARS Foster Care Database.

Toth, J. (1997). *Orphans of the Living: Stories of America's Children in Foster Care*. New York: Simon and Schuster.

Urquhart, L. R. (1989). "Separation and Loss: Assessing the Impacts on Foster Parent Retention." *Child and Adolescent Social Work*, 6, 3:193–209.

Vonk, M. E. (2001). "Cultural Competence for Transracial Adoptive Parents." *Journal of the National Association of Social Workers* 46, 3:246–55.

Wozniak, D. F. (2002). *They're All My Children: Foster Mothering in America*. New York: New York University Press.

Wright, M. A. (1998). *I'm Chocolate, You're Vanilla: Raising Healthy Black and Biracial Children in a Race-Conscious World: A Guide for Parents and Teachers*. San Francisco: Jossey-Bass.

Index